With his characteristic self-deprecating humor and pastoral warmth, Sam Allberry takes us right to the heart of the God who is triune. In these pages he has managed to combine simplicity of style with profundity of thought. It makes for compelling reading.

—**Michael Jensen,** *Lecturer in Theology and Church History at Moore College, Sydney*

Sam Allberry has returned with another characteristically fresh and readable introduction. With wry humor and solid biblical moorings, we are drawn back to marvel at the wonders of God, Father, Son, and Holy Spirit. He writes simply without being too simplistic and thus has produced a great book to put into the hands of young believers hungry to grow in their understanding and faith.

—**Mark Meynell,** *Senior Associate Minister and European Program Coordinator, All Souls, Langham Place*

Sam Allberry rightly points out how neglected the doctrine of the Trinity is, showing its importance clearly and warmly. I hope many will read this and be affected.

—**Michael Reeves,** *Head of Theology, UCCF; Author of* The Good God

This is heartwarming, awe-inspiring teaching that will fill the mind and feed the soul. Deep truths are expounded with a light touch and down-to-earth applications. Here is a book that not only will help readers to understand more deeply the mystery of God the Holy Trinity, but also moves us to worship and honor him in daily life.

—**Vaughan Roberts,** *Rector of St. Ebbe's, Oxford; Director of the Proclamation Trust*

Connected

Connected

*Living in the Light
of the Trinity*

SAM ALLBERRY

P&R
PUBLISHING
P.O. BOX 817 • PHILLIPSBURG • NEW JERSEY 08865-0817

First published in the UK by Inter-Varsity Press in 2012
North American edition issued 2013 by P&R Publishing

ISBN: 978-1-59638-595-5 (pbk)
ISBN: 978-1-59638-596-2 (Mobi)

Printed in the United States of America

Library of Congress Cataloging-in-Publication Data
Allberry, Sam.
Connected : living in the light of the Trinity / Sam Allberry. -- 1st North American ed.
pages cm.
Includes bibliographical references.
ISBN 978-1-59638-595-5 (pbk.)
1. Trinity--History of doctrines--21st century. 2. Christian life. I. Title.
BT111.3.A45 2012
231'.044--dc23
2013019642

For Fiona Ellis, Edward Nash, Amelie Lewis, and Hannah Clarke: in the hope that you will always cherish the love of God the Trinity and that this dedication makes up for forgotten birthdays.

CONTENTS

ACKNOWLEDGMENTS

WRITING ON THE TRINITY has been both an enormous joy and an enormous struggle. The joy has come from having the opportunity to think carefully about who God is. There can surely be no greater topic for reflection. Which is where the struggle comes in. I am painfully aware that the words in this book cannot do justice to the sheer wonder of God being Father, Son, and Holy Spirit.

That the project ever got to this point at all is due in no small part to the encouragement of others. Eleanor Trotter and the team at IVP continue to be a joy to work with, and I am especially grateful to Eleanor for all her patience and encouragement. Ian Thompson and Aaron Gottier at P&R have, as always, been a pleasure to work with and a great help in readying the manuscript for an American market. I now know that no one on the left-hand side of the pond has the foggiest clue what I mean when I talk about "putting the boot in" (or, for that matter, when I talk about having the "foggiest clue").

I have benefited hugely from the work and scholarship of others, especially Tim Chester, Fred Sanders, Bruce Ware, and Robert Letham, whose books on the Trinity were never far from my fingertips during this project.[1] Michael Reeves has been a terrific conversation partner, and his own book, written at the same time as this one, has already become essential reading on the Trinity.[2]

I am also grateful for the encouragement of a number of friends. Comments from Tom Watson stimulated a lot of additional thinking during the writing process. Joe Clarke, Tim Lewis, Daniel Roe, and Dan Johnson were all willing to read through the manuscript in its early stages, and I am grateful for their helpful feedback. *Connected* is a better book because of it. Needless to say, any remaining inadequacies are mine and not theirs.

Virtually all of this book has been written in the great commonwealths of Massachusetts and Virginia. Dimitri and Gay-Lynn Alldridge have coped admirably with my propensity for breaking things while staying with them, and have even invited me back. I am grateful for their friendship.

And a very special word of thanks is due to Brian and Leslie Roe, who, as well as providing the very best kinds of distraction (Brian) and carrot cake (Leslie), have encouraged me more than I can say with their enthusiasm for this project and—far more importantly—with their joyful, persevering faith in God the Trinity, even in the midst of great suffering. It is a privilege to know them.

INTRODUCTION

I AM A PRETTY POOR JUDGE of people. Some of my closest friends are individuals who, at first meeting, I would never have imagined becoming so close to one day. People I didn't think I'd click with, people with whom I had little in common, people who, where close friendship was concerned, would probably not be my "type." They had radically different interests. Or a propensity not to find my jokes funny, and to wonder why on earth I ever thought they would. Not immediately obvious friends-for-life material. But now, years later, they're friends I couldn't imagine doing without.

It turns out I can be a pretty poor judge of doctrine, too. As a young Christian I had a basic understanding that, officially, God was triune. But unofficially, it made virtually no difference to my Christian life. I prayed to God. I knew Jesus had died for my sins. I read my Bible and tried to live in a way that pleased my heavenly Father. It never really occurred to me to go any further than that. The doctrine of the Trinity was carefully filed in the drawer of "Things That All Good Christians Believe" and then never really seen again.

I had no immediate need to look further into the Trinity, and a number of suspicions were holding me back:

1. It doesn't make sense. God is one. Oh, and he's also three. Get it? Didn't think so.

2. It's not *meant* to make sense. It's just one of those things. It's not supposed to be understood. It's a mystery and we shouldn't pry. To try to analyze it in some rational, systematic way would be to miss the point. It might even spoil it. Better to leave it be; as a mystery it feels more deep when it's left that way.

3. It's too technical. To get anywhere you need to be a theologian. When you start to scratch the surface you run into a sort of multisyllabic Neverland. Ask even a basic question about the Trinity and theologians fire back answers with terms like *perichoresis*. They may as well be speaking Klingon.

4. It's embarrassing. We commend the Christian faith on the basis that it makes sense—it coheres, it's not irrational. But then someone asks us about the Trinity and we're flummoxed. It's not explainable. So we hope like crazy that it doesn't come up.

5. It's irrelevant. Assuming we bust our way through all the jargon and find some way to explain it, what are we meant to do with it? Yes, one God, three persons, but so what? What practical difference could it possibly make to my life? It looks like it will have about as much bearing on my daily life as the quadratic equations I learned at school.

I didn't seem to be alone in having these suspicions. Even people I'd heard giving talks on the Trinity gave the impression they didn't really know what to do with it. They would tell us some of the history of the doctrine. We'd get introduced to guys like Athanasius, who fought hard for the church to be clear on what the Trinity was and wasn't. (The Athanasian

Creed, for the record, uses the word *incomprehensible* a little too much for comfort, which does little to allay suspicion 2 above.) We might be given some of the technical terms. But there would be little sense of what difference the Trinity could actually make. It was hard to avoid the conclusion that, in the memorable words of Michael Reeves, the Trinity was a doctrine we might never have had if a bunch of theologians long ago had had girlfriends.[1]

Such thinking comes to an abrupt and happy halt the moment we begin to look more closely at what the Bible shows us about the Trinity.

It really does make sense. It adds up. (Pun intended.) God wants us to understand what he is like. We don't need to learn a new language or start smoking a pipe to get our heads around it. We just need to come humbly and prayerfully to the Scriptures.

And what a difference it makes. Sinclair Ferguson highlights one of the ways we see the practical significance of the Trinity:

> I've often reflected on the rather obvious thought that when his disciples were about to have the world collapse in on them, our Lord spent so much time in the Upper Room speaking to them about the mystery of the Trinity. If anything could underline the necessity of Trinitarianism for practical Christianity, that must surely be it![2]

Understanding the Trinity helps us make sense of so much of what we hold dear: friendship, marriage, church, love, service, identity. Things that are precious to us, but which we are not always able to properly account for, find new significance when examined in the light of the Trinity. Things we cherish about God—his love and integrity, the coherence of his Word, the nearness of his presence, and above all his matchless love poured out for us through the death of Christ—all these can only make real sense when we discover that God is, in fact, triune.

One of the great privileges of pastoral ministry is being able to set yourself particular subjects to study and teach about. I find this the best way to respond to areas of Christian truth and the Bible on which I need to do more thinking, setting myself the task of doing a bit of in-depth teaching on it. Nothing like a deadline to sharpen the mind! So a few years ago I set myself the task of giving a series of talks on the Trinity, and I have attempted to teach on this subject a number of times since. My approach has been the same as for any other area of biblical truth: try to teach it the way the Bible does, to the extent that the Bible does and for the reasons that the Bible does.

The Bible, of course, doesn't use the word *Trinity*. You won't find it in Old or New Testament. But there's a difference between the word being absent and the concept being absent. *Trinity* is merely the term Christians have adopted to capture the fact that the one God has shown himself to be three persons. It sums up his three-in-oneness, his tri-unity.

And very few passages are actually "about" the Trinity. It is not as if Paul sets aside a chapter or so of a letter to hash it all out. No verse starts with, "Now about the Trinity, folks, here's what you really need to know . . ." The closest we get to this is the extended sections of Jesus' teaching in John's gospel, particularly John 14–17. Most of the time when it comes up, the Trinity is an essential background to the main point of a passage while not itself being that main point. It's like a prominent local building: pretty much always in view, but for most of the time not actually the thing you are looking at. Most of the insights we are given about the Trinity in Scripture come on the back of insights we are being given about something else. The Great Commission in Matthew 28 is not about the Trinity. It is about Jesus sending out disciple-making disciples. But really we can't understand *that* without making reference to the Trinity.

Despite my early impressions, the doctrine of the Trinity has become a dear friend. Far from being an irrelevance or a burden, it is a truth and a reality I now could not bear to be without. It is no exaggeration to say that, apart from my conversion, studying the Trinity has had a greater spiritual impact on me than anything else in my life. God is far bigger and more beautiful than I could ever have realized.

PART 1
THE TRINITY AND GOD

1

GOD: THE BOTTOM LINE

God Is One: Part 1

IT ALL BEGAN WITH a question: "One of the teachers of the law came and heard them debating. Noticing that Jesus had given them a good answer, he asked him, 'Of all the commandments, which is the most important?'" (Mark 12:28).

We can't be sure precisely why he asked. He seems to have been impressed with Jesus' debating skills. Jesus has just acquitted himself well before a delegation of Sadducees, seeing them off with some deft use of Old Testament Scripture, so he clearly has some game. Let's try him on the commandments and see how he fares.

The question may also reflect some genuine bewilderment. Jewish lawyers had enumerated 613 separate commandments within Old Testament law. Like someone overwhelmed by too much information, this man may have been looking to Jesus for some guidance, a sense of what really mattered most to God. Jesus seemed to possess some uncommon insight. "What's the bottom line here? Which commandment is the most important?"

Whatever the motivation behind the question, Jesus leads in with a quotation from Deuteronomy. But he does something unexpected. He was asked for a commandment, but he opens with a truth about God: " 'The most important one,' answered Jesus, 'is this: "Hear, O Israel, the Lord our God, the Lord is one" ' " (Mark 12:29).

Doctrine comes before ethics, confession before commandment. Before assessing what you need to do for God comes an understanding of who that God is.

And that God is one. This is the bottom line, the foundation. Everything else—including how he wants us to live—will need to flow from this context. Discipleship (following God) has to follow theology (knowing God). And the particular characteristic of God that Jesus puts front and center is his oneness. This is the truth about God that precedes everything else. It may be a subtle rebuke to Jesus' conversation partner: God's oneness makes trying to pick one commandment over another a moot point. They're not independent options on a menu; the same God stands behind them all.

This is where we need to start. God is one. It may be a short phrase, but it is packed with an explosive charge: God is one means that God is unique.

In the West, we're familiar with the concept of there being one God. It is the God most people would have in their mind: a unique, one-of-a-kind God. You believe in a God or you don't believe in a God. Whatever else people in the West might believe, if God comes into the equation, there tends to be only one of him.

Not so in the ancient world. While the norm in the West has been to believe (or not) in one God, the ancient world was proud of its polytheism. There were different gods for different things: you would have a god of travel or commerce or sport. In fact, the more gods the better—you stood a greater chance of covering all your bases. It was the equivalent of that episode of *The Simpsons* in which Homer, believing he is about to die, cries out in desperation, "Jesus! Allah! Buddha!—I love you all!" That was the kind of setup they had in the ancient world. Hedge your bets; believe in as many gods as possible. It was the fashion. To believe in one unique God, as Jews and Christians did, was dorky.

The Bible has always insisted on monotheism: there is only one God. The verse Jesus quoted from Deuteronomy 6 was not plucked from scriptural obscurity; it was one of the foundational verses for the people of God in the Old Testament. It was said every day, morning and evening. Nor was it a lone verse in standing for God's uniqueness. Far from being a theological "blip" in the Bible, Deuteronomy 6 is in fact typical of many passages affirming God's uniqueness. Consider some of the others:

This truth was never intended to be just a matter of mathematical fact.

> I am the LORD, and there is no other;
>> apart from me there is no God.
> I will strengthen you,
>> though you have not acknowledged me,
> so that from the rising of the sun
>> to the place of its setting
> men may know there is none besides me.
>> I am the LORD, and there is no other. (Isa. 45:5–6)

This truth was never intended to be just a matter of mathematical fact. It's not like being able to number how many states there are in the United States or how many players make up a football team or how many planets there are in the solar system.[1] It is a truth that makes an enormous practical difference. It applies to us in any number of ways, but two stand out in particular: devotion and mission.

DEVOTION

God's uniqueness compels us to wholehearted devotion. If God is one, then our devotion to him must be total. Consider the logic of the verses Jesus quotes.

> Hear O Israel, the Lord our God, the Lord is one. Love the Lord your God with all your heart and with all your soul and with all your mind and with all your strength. (Mark 12:29–30)

The observation that God is one is not incidental to what follows. It is the grounds for it. The Lord our God is one. *Therefore* we are to love him with all that we are and all that we have. His oneness and the totality of our love for him are tightly bound together. If God were anything other than one, we would not need to love him with our "all." Someone doing two jobs part-time could not be expected to give the entirety of their working life to one of their two bosses. But God's oneness means he deserves our everything.

In other words, we must not compartmentalize God—give him *some* of our heart, *some* of our soul; split our mind and strength between him and four or five other claimants. Yet this is so easily done. We allow God some parts of our lives but not others. I say he can have my Sundays but not my Saturdays, my church life but not my social life, my work but not my wallet, my industry but not my fantasy. For each of us there will be particular areas of our lives that we instinctively want to rope off from God.

Out of bounds

I love having people over to my house. But the half hour before they arrive tends to involve me frantically trying to make the place approximately presentable. A principle which has helped me greatly in this is to think of tidying up not as *getting rid of* a mess, but as *putting it somewhere else*. So the spare room upstairs becomes the dumping ground. The week's accumulated debris is scooped up and banished there. Actually putting it all away would take too much time and would require a system for where everything goes. So the room upstairs takes it all. And, once the guests have left, it all gets transferred back downstairs again.

The corollary of all of this is that, while everywhere else in the house is open to guests, the spare room is not. The door to that room remains firmly closed. If I could get my hands on some, I'd cover the doorway with that yellow police tape they use to cordon off crime scenes.

It works with houseguests. And so we think it will also work with God. I'll have certain areas of my life specially tidied up for his appreciation. Others remain strictly off-limits. God is very welcome in some areas, but not in all.

But because God is one, we can't brush him off like that. It's why the quotation from Jesus begins the way it does. If you're thinking you might follow him, you need to know that it's got to be all or nothing. He deserves all of my life, all my heart, soul, mind, and strength. And the truth is that I need him in all of my life. There is no corner of my heart, soul, mind, or strength where his presence would not be a huge blessing.

Where the demons get it right

Failure to grasp this is very serious indeed. James wrote a letter to Christians struggling at this very point. Many of them seemed to think they could blend following God with following the ways of this world, giving God part of themselves but not all. Spiritually they were being disingenuous. James called them "double-minded." In today's language we would call them "two-faced."

James exposes their hypocrisy. They profess to follow one God, but their lifestyle demonstrates otherwise. And so James calls them on it: "You believe that there is one God. Good! Even the demons believe that—and shudder!" (James 2:19). This is tragic. On this point of the creed it turns out that the demons have got more consistent theology than the Christians have. Not a great position to be in—getting theologically trumped by demons, of all things. The demons know very well that God is one. And at least in their case, you can tell because they shudder: their belief is evident. But for James' readers it is not so. They are really leading only part-Christian lives. James has called their bluff. Their half-hearted faith shows that their God is not worthy of everything. He is not the God who is one. Their faith is dead, their response to God woeful. They are unfaithful.

A couple have got married. It has been a long, painful process getting to this point. The bride has not been, shall we say, entirely straightforward. The groom has hung in there—hung in with her tantrums, her inconsistencies, and even her infidelities. And now, at long last, they are man and wife.

It is a few weeks later. The boxes are now all unpacked. The last of the thank-you notes has been sent off. It feels like home. Familiarity. Our groom has managed to leave work early and, ever the romantic, picks up some flowers on the way home. He doesn't spot the unfamiliar car parked across the street, nor the jacket that is not his hanging in the hall. It is only when he enters the bedroom that it all becomes clear.

Adultery. It's a horrific picture, but one sadly not unfamiliar in our world today.

And that is the picture that best captures what we're doing spiritually when we give God only a portion of our affection. James does not sugarcoat it for us: "You adulterous people, don't you know that friendship with the world is hatred towards God? Anyone who chooses to be a friend of the world becomes an enemy of God" (James 4:4).

It is a situation we need to repent of. James calls us to come back to God. To recognize the abhorrence of what we've done when we've not given him our all. To be brokenhearted. To weep. Some sins warrant our tears. It astonishes me how quickly I will well up at a sentimental movie and yet how slowly I am moved to tears by my own sin.

We need to remember that God is one. He deserves our all. And, amazingly, when we do draw near to him again he draws near to us, washing us afresh in his grace and mercy.

MISSION

God's uniqueness also compels Christian mission. His oneness is linked directly in Scripture to the mandate to call on all peoples to come to him. It is the lens through which we need to view other belief systems.

Corinth was a place with tons of different gods. Like an enormous food court, the choice was vast and bewildering; the temptation was to pick and mix whatever took your spiritual fancy. A little Kung Pow chicken here, a little lamb tagine there.

In this context the early Christians were understandably cautious. A particular concern was that they might get spiritually contaminated through accidental contact with stuff associated with some of these other gods. Tim Chester encourages us to put ourselves in their shoes. Imagine you are having supper in Corinth with your pagan friends from across the street. You're enjoying a lovely meal, only to discover that the meat you've been eating had earlier been pledged to a pagan god.[2] What would you do? Carry on eating with your fingers crossed? Immediately spit the food out and do your best to retrieve the rest? Or ask for another helping without a care?

Paul had two things to say in response to their concerns.

No God but one

"So then, about eating food sacrificed to idols: We know that an idol is nothing at all in the world and that there is no God but one" (1 Cor. 8:4).

The first thing to note is that idols are nothing at all. Those other gods being worshipped by the pagan neighbours across the street aren't actually real. They don't exist except in the minds of those who worship them. There is no God but one. Paul continues: "For even if there are so-called gods, whether in heaven or on earth (as indeed there are many 'gods' and many 'lords'), yet for us there is but one God" (1 Cor. 8:5–6).

If the God of the gospel is one, then all other gods are nothing in this world. They are just "so-called" gods. God's oneness excludes all other supposed contenders. Jupiter is not real. Vishnu is not real. None of them are.

This is not to say that there is nothing there at all. Paul goes on to tell us later in the letter that there are demons behind these alternate deities. But the key point here is that the gods themselves do not actually exist.

This has massive implications for how we are to understand the non-Christian beliefs of our friends and neighbors. We're not to think that Vishnu is out there somewhere, even in an inferior position to the God of the Bible. Vishnu exists objectively nowhere outside the minds of those who believe in Vishnu. Vishnu is only a "so-called" god. Demonic forces are certainly there, misleading worshippers of Vishnu; Vishnu himself is not, and the same can be said of any other spiritual objects of worship reverenced by our friends.

This is not to say we should be flippant with our friends about this. Indeed, we need to take care how we articulate our faith. But we do need to be very clear in our own minds: there is but one God.

This has always been the testimony of Scripture. Consider the opening words of Psalm 96:

> Sing to the LORD a new song;
>   sing to the LORD, all the earth.
> Sing to the LORD, praise his name;
>   proclaim his salvation day after day.
> Declare his glory among the nations,
>   his marvellous deeds among all peoples.
> For great is the LORD and most worthy of praise;
>   he is to be feared above all gods.
> For all the gods of the nations are idols,
>   but the LORD made the heavens. (Ps. 96:1–5)

God's people are called to sing his praises. So far so good. But notice that they're not to do so in a holy huddle, sequestered away from the rest of society, but among the peoples. The pagans around were to hear the excellencies of God being proclaimed and sung by his people. The purpose was not to annoy them or get in their face. It was to be an invitation to those same peoples to come to know this God and praise him for themselves (as verse 7 says).

The rationale for all this has already been made clear by the psalmist:

> For great is the LORD and most worthy of praise;
>   he is to be feared above all gods.

> For all the gods of the nations are idols,
> but the LORD made the heavens. (Ps. 96:4–5)

There is only one God, one creator, one Lord. The psalm again reminds us that these other gods worshipped by the nations are none other than "idols"—literally, "nothings." God's oneness precludes the existence of any other deity. It also reminds us of the corollary, that this one God is to be commended to all.

One God for all

To see this we need to head from Corinth over to Rome.

Some of the Jewish Christians in Paul's day were greatly concerned about some of the implications of his gospel. They had grown accustomed to people from other backgrounds becoming culturally Jewish in order to convert to faith in God. It was part of the "package" of works they presumed necessary to being made right with God. But Paul has been explaining that, through the death of Jesus, *anyone* can be justified by faith. Jewish culture has nothing to do with it. Through the cross, individuals of any cultural background can come straight to God. God's people can now be multicultural. You don't need to become Jewish to become Christian; no circumcision is necessary!

As Paul unpacks what it means to be justified by faith, he anticipates the objections of some of these Jewish Christians. His response is simple and very pointed: they have forgotten God's oneness.

> Is God the God of the Jews only? Is he not the God of Gentiles too? Yes, of Gentiles too, since there is only one God, who will justify the circumcised by faith, and the uncircumcised through that same faith. (Rom. 3:29–30)

God is the God of all people. Paul fires out a couple of rhetorical questions: You really think God is God just of the Jews? He's the God of the Gentiles too, right? And, just in case they get the second one wrong, Paul steps in and answers it himself: Yes, God of the Gentiles too; God of them all, not just the Jews, and because he is the God of all peoples and cultures, they all come to him on the exact same basis, irrespective of background or culture. We all get right with God the same way: through the life, death, and resurrection of Jesus.

This is something we need to hear today. We can easily fall into the same trap as those Jewish Christians, by implying, for example, through our church practice that you have to become like "us" in order to be a Christian. We would never say that—in fact, we'd probably never even consciously think it—but it is very easy to imply.

Our way of doing things in church probably reflects the sub-culture from which the church has grown or to which the majority of the congregation belongs. We probably don't even notice the extent to which the life of the church reflects "our way" of doing things. But the message to everybody else can unwittingly be that they need to become like us to become Christian, that the great God of Scripture is only the God of people like us.

I suspect this is a blind spot for many of us. It is all too easy for our cultural practice to feel like the norm, to assume it's just the obvious and right way of doing things. I come from a white, English, middle-class background, as do the majority of people at my church. Now there's nothing wrong with that. But our locality is becoming increasingly diverse. There are growing communities of people from south Asia and Eastern Europe. We therefore need to be careful not to imply that our way is *the* way to be if you want to be a Christian around here.

It might be the style of music, or the amount of emotional openness we consider to be normal, or the extent to which we build deep relationships with one another that conveys this. It might even be the level of literacy our congregational life assumes of those participating. Are we willing to hold loosely to these things for the sake of reaching and involving those from other cultural backgrounds? Do we resist the change in "feel" that would result from having a culturally broader church family? Will we try to accommodate them or just assimilate them?

Or we could put it Paul's way: is God just the God of people like us? Or of others too? There is only one God. And his one gospel is for all peoples.

We can begin to see why, when asked which was the most important commandment, Jesus answered in the way he did. Foundational to everything involved in following him is the understanding that he is one. As we double-click on that concept, we begin to see how much flows from it. "God is One" means that God deserves our all. Wholehearted Christian devotion stems from this. And "God is one" also means that God is unique. The heartbeat of Christian mission is the conviction that there is no God but one, and the gospel of this one God is for all.

2

DIVINE INTEGRITY

God Is One: Part 2

ONE OF THE MORE memorable conversations I had with my grandmother as a child concerned what my dad had been like as a young man. Quite apart from the shock of discovering that he actually *was* a young man was the added surprise of discovering what *kind* of young man he had been. It was quite a revelation. He had played drums for a local band called Slash Wildly and the Cut-throats which, at its height, boasted literally half-dozens of followers. When he wasn't tearing up the villages of western Kent with the Cut-throats, he was apparently tearing around on a motorcycle. This was quite a lot for my young head to get around—my *dad* on a motorcycle! It was a whole side to him I had never known about. There was more to him than I had ever realized.

We are never done getting to know God, never at the point where there will be no more surprises. One of the thrills of being a Christian is discovering ever greater depths to his being and character. And as we continue to mine ever deeper into the seam of his oneness, we continue to find that there is more and more to him than we might ever have realized.

"The Lord is one" tells us far more than a mathematical truth: that there happens to be one of him—not two or four or twelve. It tells us something else. The Hebrew word for "one" in the mini-creed from Deuteronomy has a particular color to it. It means more than being digitally singular. It speaks of there being a unity to God, that he is undivided. He is one: there is an integrity to him. No contradiction and no inconsistency. All he is, desires, says, and does is of a piece. It holds together. All of it fits perfectly. There is a consistency to everything about God.

Everything else we go on to learn about God's nature has to be understood within this context. Whatever we go on to discover about God being triune will not in any way contradict this. Our consideration of what it means for him to be three persons must happen within the framework of his complete unity and oneness.

Understanding God's unity will have significant implications for how we view him, how we think about the death of Jesus, and how we live our lives as Christians.

OUR VIEW OF GOD

As we come to understand God as being three persons—Father, Son, and Holy Spirit—we need to keep in mind that these persons exist in complete unity. And that means we can't have one person of the Trinity without the others. Many wrong views of God are immediately straightened out once we grasp this.

You cannot have one without the others

God is three persons. But these persons are one God,

distinct from one another but remaining united. They cannot be separated.

There's a trick many of us used with our parents when we were growing up.[1] We wanted something—an extra treat, to stay up late, to go out somewhere—so we went and asked the nearest parent. They said no. So what did we do? Went to find the other parent before they found out that a parental ruling had already been made on the matter. If Mom says no, maybe Dad will say yes. We just need to get to him before Mom does.

We can achieve a measure of success with this when it comes to our parents. But it never works with the persons of the Trinity. You can't run to the Son, hoping he will grant what the Father has denied. They are one. You can't fall out with the Son and still think you can get in with God the Father.

This might seem obvious, but I've met many people who think they can do just that. People who don't "do Jesus" but say they believe in God and that this is all that matters. I recently had a conversation with an elderly window-cleaner who made this very point. He had stormed the beaches of Normandy on D-Day. It was sad to have to say to such an honorable man that he was wrong on a matter as weighty as this. If it had been just my opinion, he could have dismissed it. But it is the clear testimony of Scripture: you cannot have God the Father without God the Son. "No-one who denies the Son has the Father"(1 John 2:23). They exist in perfect unity.

Rejecting the Son means that you are nowhere with God at all.

This means, ultimately, that people who don't believe in Jesus don't actually believe in the God who is there. To reject Jesus is to reject the Father whom he perfectly reveals. Jews who reject Jesus as the Christ don't really believe in the God of Scripture.

We mustn't think that they are somehow "half in" just because they claim to follow the God of the Old Testament. For someone to reject Jesus shows they do not really believe in the Father either. Rejecting the Son means that you are nowhere with God at all.

You cannot play the persons of the Trinity off against one another

I've heard people try to match up different kinds of church with different persons of the Trinity, as if you pick the person you like the best and construct a church around what you think he's into.

It's like fans of the boy band One Direction who like to subdivide into whether you're a "Harry fan" or a Niall fan" at heart. (I've no idea who the other ones are.) Christians will sometimes define themselves by particular persons of the Trinity. So some will say that Catholic and Orthodox churches are really into God the Father, focusing on his remoteness and transcendence. Evangelical churches are the ones that are all about God the Son. And the charismatics/Pentecostals are the Spirit fans. And, so the thinking goes, if we can just get all these churches to mingle a bit more, introducing each to the other persons of the Trinity, then—presto!—we'll all get a more balanced experience of God. Church ecumenism then becomes the goal, uniting the denominations the means of putting Humpty back together again.

It might all sound attractive: Unite the church! Get all of God! But it overlooks something which is not incidental. God is one. You're not truly engaging with any one person of the Trinity without engaging with them all. If you think the Son is at your church while the Father is down the street at the one with all the incense and the Spirit is at that one across town with the bean bags and lava lamps, then in all likelihood none of these churches is actually having true fellowship with the "real" God at all. The Trinity is not like a band whose members occasionally take time out from one another to pursue solo careers. The persons of the Godhead are not like the cast of that hit ensemble TV show who are all trying to carve out their own movie careers during the summer hiatus. God is one. You relate to the Trinity or you don't relate to God at all.

> You relate to the Trinity or you don't relate to God at all.

You cannot "balance" the persons of the Trinity

It's 2003. I'm in a training seminar for church leaders on the relationship between theology and ministry. Toward the end of his presentation, the speaker wraps things up with this statement: "The Word without the Spirit will dry you up; the Spirit without the Word will blow you up." Many heads nod to confirm that this is indubitably so. One or two recall instances where they saw this in practice. Heads nod more vigorously.[2] I feel uneasy. I hate moments like this. Everyone else seems to love what's being said, but something doesn't feel quite right and I can't put my finger on why.

It is some time, and further study, before the penny drops.[3] The statement implies the need for a balance between the Spirit and the Word, as if the two are somehow heading in different directions and need the moderating influence of each other. Such thinking misunderstands what both the Word and the Spirit are in themselves. The Word of God is not a dry, dusty thing that has the effect of an industrial-strength dehumidifier. The Word of God, truly apprehended, is incendiary: "My heart grew hot within me, and as I meditated, the fire burned" (Ps. 39:3); "Were not our hearts burning within us while he talked with us on the road and opened the Scriptures to us?" (Luke 24:32). Nor is the Spirit some chaotic force that charges about like a young child who's had too many Cocoa Puffs for breakfast. He is the Spirit of truth after all,[4] whose fruit is self-control.

This thinking also misunderstands how the Word and the Spirit relate to each other. They are not opposing forces in need of balance. In the Bible, Word and Spirit come together as speech and breath: "All Scripture," Paul tells us, "is God-breathed" (2 Tim. 3:16). The relationship between the Word and the Spirit is like a happy marriage. It's nothing like an adolescent couple who are forever breaking up and getting back together again. As Tim Chester says, "We cannot talk of the Spirit's work apart from the Word of God, nor can we think of the Word of God apart from the work of the Spirit."[5]

But above all it misunderstands the fact that God is one. No two elements of his work are ever in tension or contradiction.

OUR VIEW OF THE CROSS

We also need to apply the truth of God's oneness to how we think about the death of Jesus.

Was the Father reluctant?

It is easy to get the wrong impression about what was going on when Jesus died, thinking that perhaps either the Father or the Son might not have been quite as much on board as the other. Some might think, for example, that Jesus had to twist the Father's arm in order to save us. It was almost as if Jesus sneaked down here and died for our sins so that the Father had virtually no choice but to accept us. Thank goodness Jesus stepped in and calmed him down.

We do not need to look very far to see how wrong this way

of thinking is. When Jesus first steps onto the scene in Mark's gospel, it is to receive the baptism of John the Baptist. The whole episode acts as a commissioning for the ministry Jesus is about to undertake:

> At that time Jesus came from Nazareth in Galilee and was baptised by John in the Jordan. As Jesus was coming up out of the water, he saw heaven being torn open and the Spirit descending on him like a dove. And a voice came from heaven: "You are my Son, whom I love; with you I am well pleased." (Mark 1:9–11)

This is a wonderful scene of the Trinity in action. Jesus is going forward for baptism, the Spirit is descending, and the Father is speaking. (If nothing else, this shoots down the idea that the Father, Son, and Spirit are all just different roles or modes that God switches between.)

Notice the significance of the baptism Jesus is receiving. Mark has already described it as "a baptism of repentance for the forgiveness of sins" (Mark 1:4). The crowds pouring into the Judean countryside to receive this baptism were doing so as an expression of their need for forgiveness. This is the baptism Jesus, the sinless one, himself goes forward for. He is standing in the place of sinners.

The descent of the Spirit on him indicates that this is the moment at which Jesus is formally beginning his ministry, the very ministry that will take him to the cross and the ultimate standing in the place of sinners. It is for this that the Spirit empowers him. It's a foretaste of the way in which, by that same Spirit, Jesus will offer up his life as a sacrifice for sin.[6] It's also a foretaste of what that death will achieve. As Jesus rises from his baptism, the heavens are torn open. As he later dies on the cross (a death he refers to as "my baptism," Mark 10:38), the temple curtain is torn apart, indicating that the way to God is open for us.

But as well as the empowering of God the Spirit, we see the deep approval of God the Father. In setting his face to fulfill this task, Jesus is pleasing the Father who sent him. The Father was more than "in on it"; he was the initiator of the whole plan in the first place. None of this was taking place without his full approval or initiative.

Was the Son reluctant?

Others seem to speak of the cross in a way that suggests that it was Jesus, not the Father, who was not fully on board. God's anger at sin is sometimes likened to a runaway semitruck hurtling towards a helpless crowd of people, until, at the final moment, the driver yanks the wheel and swerves the truck into his son instead. Or sometimes people talk about the cross as though Jesus were some hapless third party who happened to blunder into the scene. Or that Jesus was almost unknowingly co-opted by the Father to bear the punishment that had to fall somewhere. There he was, minding his own business, when out of the blue the whole gamut of God's wrath fell upon him.

There is so much wrong with this kind of thinking—not least in implying that the Father is somehow unable to control his own emotions. It is wrong to suggest that the Son is a victim in the whole affair.

The picture we have in the Gospels is very different. Jesus is fully aware of the cross that awaits him in Jerusalem. More than that, he is determined to face it. One of the most striking examples of this determination comes at the midpoint in Mark's gospel:

He then began to teach them that the Son of Man must suffer many things and be rejected by the elders, chief priests and teachers of the law, and that he must be killed and after three days rise again. He spoke plainly about this, and Peter took him aside and began to rebuke him.

But when Jesus turned and looked at his disciples, he rebuked Peter. "Get behind me, Satan!" he said. "You do not have in mind the things of God, but the things of men." (Mark 8:31–33)

It is a key moment. For the first time Jesus has been correctly identified as the Christ. His identity has been understood. He now moves on to a new subject ("he *began* to teach," Mark 8:31): his purpose in coming. Jesus insists that he must suffer, die, and rise again. He *must* suffer these things. Not "might" but "must." Jesus was not saying that a violent death at the hands of the authorities was likely, but that it was imperative. His death would not be terribly bad luck but the intentional climax of his mission.

Peter is not impressed by this. Yes, Jesus is the Christ, but he doesn't seem to have read the script: dying is not a Christ-type thing to do. And so he takes Jesus to one side and rebukes him.

And Jesus, in turn, rebukes Peter. Notice how he does it—in front of everyone and in the strongest possible terms: "Get behind me, *Satan.*"

Jesus' point is this: his death is not incidental but central to his mission. To be opposed to it is to be on the side of the devil himself. If you are not with me on this, Peter, you are not with me on anything. Jesus is determined to die.

What we see from all this, then, is that the Father and the Son are at one in this plan. Neither is unwilling. Both are utterly committed. And, as we have also seen, the Spirit too is fully involved, empowering Jesus to face the cross and offer up his life to the Father. To teach or imply otherwise is to deny the oneness of God.

OUR VIEW OF THE CHRISTIAN LIFE

So what is our response to God in light of his unity? If God himself is integrated, then it stands to reason that his word to us is too. It is of a piece; it hangs together and coheres perfectly.

It is important to recognize this and not to read into God some of our own less attractive traits. If you were to collect up all the things I have ever spoken and written (poor you), then you would quickly discover that they do not all fit together. There will be things on which I have changed my mind over time. Sadly there will also be things that I said in the context of one group that contradict things said in another group. Indeed, many of my words would be seen to reflect a fickleness on my part.

We are not consistent. God is three persons who in their unity are one; I am one person who through my sinful nature is fragmented and split. By nature, none of us can be truly consistent with ourselves.

Our God is wonderfully different. By nature he is one, and so all his words fit together into a coherent whole. There is complete integrity to all he has said to us, something that must impact on our view of the Christian life.

Obedience in one area as an excuse for disobedience in another

We can't use obedience in one area of the Christian life as an excuse for disobedience in another. To do so implies some sort of tension within God's Word, as if what one part calls us to do involves setting aside what another part calls us to do. If this ever seems to us to be the case, then it means we have misunderstood God's Word or else we are using this supposed inconsistency as an excuse for not doing what we know God wants us to do.

We see an example of this in the time of Jesus.[7] In one of his run-ins with the Pharisees, Jesus chided them for not fulfilling God's command to honor their parents. They were not making adequate provision for them. Their excuse? They were trying to devote themselves to the cause of God. Money that should have been given to their parents was instead being "dedicated to God." Jesus did not mince his words. They may have claimed to have been honoring God in this way, but in reality it was just rank disobedience: "You nullify the word of God" (Mark 7:13). Sadly, this was just one of "many such things" they did. Any supposed act of honoring God that involves going against what he has said elsewhere is going to be wrong. God's Word never contradicts itself in that way.

It is easy to think of ways in which we act like those Pharisees today. I think of a young believer I know, living in a somewhat dysfunctional family, who uses the biblical principle of encouraging other believers as an excuse to spend as much time as possible at church meetings and as little time as possible at home. Whatever it might mean to obey the command for Christians to "encourage one another" (Heb. 10:25), it won't be at the expense of our requirement to honor our families.

Or I think of the Christian I know who is in the habit of getting drunk with his non-Christian friends, insisting it is okay to do so because God wants him to be "in the world." There is some truth here: God does want us to take an active place in the life of this world. But that is no reason to join in activities that Scripture explicitly forbids.[8]

Or I think of myself and the times when I neglect an awkward but needy church member because I think of some other (more preferable) aspect of the work that needs doing. It can sound plausible when I explain it to others, but in my heart I know that I am excusing disobedience in one area by pleading obedience in another. And by doing so I am treating God's word as if it were schizophrenic. We will never need to sin in one area in order to obey in another.

Obedience in one area as a threat to obedience in another

Another more subtle form of this is when we fear that obedience in one area will threaten obedience in another. Perhaps unintentionally, we end up pitting two biblical imperatives against each other as though they were in competition and we needed to pick which one we should focus on.

A pastor explains that he is uninterested in the quality of the music at his church because he worries that it will somehow undermine the importance of the preaching. This is a false dichotomy. To think that one threatens the other means that one (or both) have not been properly understood.

Another example is when Christians worry that concerning themselves with the practical needs of their community constitutes a possible threat to evangelism. We are all called to share our faith. Paul speaks of letting our "conversation be seasoned with salt," and Peter speaks of the need to be prepared to "answer everyone who asks you" to give a reason for your faith.[9] We are also called to "do good to all" and to do practical good to others, especially to those most materially in need of help.[10] Both speaking of Christ to others and caring for the needs of the poor should be concerns of all Christians. Neither is an intrinsic threat to the other. God, after all, is one.

That God is one was the foundational creed for the Old Testament people of God, and it remains the truth we need to grasp in order to live for that same God today. Faithful discipleship will follow faithful doctrine. Understanding God is essential for being able to follow him. He is the one God of all creation, warranting our wholehearted devotion and commitment to his mission. And he is the God who is one—whose perfect integrity

Faithful discipleship will follow faithful doctrine.

and unity undergird all that he is and does. If we do not understand this divine integrity, we will easily slip into wrong thinking about God, salvation, and our response to him.

3

THE ONE WHO IS THREE

God as Trinity: Part 1

IT WAS HER PARENTS who had chosen her name. But a federal judge ruled that—despite her young age—she should be allowed to change it. Her name, he concluded, "makes a fool out of this child" and would be a "social disability." Her name, after all, was Talula Does the Hula From Hawaii.[1]

We have a curious relationship with our names. In one sense, they don't matter a great deal. A name is just a label. A couple of syllables or so. We need to have something that people can yell to get our attention.

Often it was chosen for us on quite a simple basis: a name our parents liked the sound of or one that had a particular association or family connection. We might just as easily have been called something else. Up until the day I was born, I was going to be named William, but once I arrived my mother felt that I was a Sam, and thus I was so named. (My father had responded to my arrival by swiftly passing out and so may not have been available for comment.) But I doubt if being named William rather than Sam would have altered much.[2]

But in other ways our names matter to us a great deal. A name is far more than just a convenient label to slap on someone. It is bound up with his identity. Our names are who we are. I am *Sam*, not someone else. I am glad not to be a William—no offense to any Williams out there; it's just not me.

This is why we usually dislike it when someone messes up our name. Something arrives addressed to us with our name misspelt, or someone mistakes our name for something else or even plain forgets it altogether. If you get my name wrong, it is as if you have got *me* wrong. It is also why we are so attuned to our names. I can be in a crowded and noisy supermarket, but my ears will immediately prick up if, somewhere in all that background cacophony, someone uses my name. Names matter.

When Jesus commanded his followers to baptize future disciples, he said they should be baptized into a name—a name they would thereafter be publicly identified with, a name that summed up the new life his new followers were now beginning. This was who they now were. It was what they were now about. They were now bound up with the God identified by this name. And this God is, we discover, three persons, all bearing this one name in which Jesus' disciples are to be baptized: "Therefore go and make disciples of all nations, baptising them in the name of the Father and of the Son and of the Holy Spirit" (Matt. 28:19). Following Jesus means becoming involved in the Trinity.

The Trinity describes the Christian name for God. To borrow from Fred Sanders, it is "God's way of being God."[3] When we come to Jesus, the Trinity is the reality into which he leads us. It provides the framework and rationale for our discipleship, the context for properly understanding who Jesus is and why he came.

Coming to Jesus opens up this reality to us, and going on with him deepens our understanding of it. Following Jesus and understanding the Trinity are inextricably linked. To embrace and understand the trinitarian nature of God is not going to confuse us in our walk with Christ or distract us from the priorities his gospel gives us. Quite the opposite. Understanding the Trinity will serve only to enhance our grasp of who God is and illuminate the contours of the very gospel we seek to believe.

GOD AS TRINITY IN THE OLD TESTAMENT

When Jesus speaks of God in this way, he is not putting some new spin on things. This is no innovation on his part. In declaring God to be Trinity he is not debuting an entirely novel way of thinking about God. It is not a rabbit he's pulled out of his theological hat. The Trinity has always been who God is. Jesus is shedding light on something God has always said about himself, something that has always been true of him.

A number of years ago I moved into a new apartment. This was the first time I'd properly had my own place and, since it was unfurnished, there was a lot I needed to buy as I settled in. I consequently set out to the nearest large department store to pick up some furniture. It wasn't long before I started to experience shopping fatigue and started to look around for a distraction. I soon found it. On the far wall of the vast shop floor, I saw an image that immediately grabbed my attention. *Darth Vader.*

I was immediately transfixed. Instinctively I headed over to have a proper look.

As I approached I became aware that there was something unusual about this image, something I couldn't quite put my finger on. It was only when I was much nearer that I realized what had made it seem so odd from a distance. It was a mosaic. The image of Vader was made up of hundreds of stills from the original *Star Wars* trilogy. Right up close it was just rows of small pictures, but as you backed off you began to see the outline and image of the Sith Lord. It was not just a simple image—there was a complexity to it. Needless to say, I bought it right away. Posters like that are what they invented walls for.

We have seen that God is one. He alone is God. He is unique. And there is a perfect integrity to all he is, does, and says. Perfect unity.

But as we get closer to this God, as we move closer for a better look—or, more precisely, as Scripture unfolds and he begins to reveal himself more fully—we begin to see that there is a complexity to his oneness. It has a dynamic, a dimension we may not have noticed from a distant glance.

This complexity to God's oneness is something we see from the very earliest pages of Scripture. Throughout the Old Testament there are hints and suggestions that God's oneness is not flat or monolithic.

The plurality of God

The opening verses of the Bible describe God's work of creation. When God comes to make humanity, there is a moment of deliberation that is very revealing. "Then God said, 'Let us make man in our image, in our likeness'"(Gen. 1:26).

As God reflects to himself on this particular act of creation, he does so in the plural. Not "Let *me* make . . . in *my* image," but "Let *us* make . . . in *our* image." This one God speaks of himself as an "us," not a "me." There is plurality.

Some have suggested that the "we" is not just directed at God himself but includes the heavenly host of angels. But whatever roles angels may have in executing God's plans, they are not co-creators with God, and in any case we human beings are not made in their image. We are made in God's image alone. And the God in whose image we are made is "us." The most natural reading is the obvious one: God is reflecting a plurality within his being.

Nor is this passage a one-off. Consider the following two instances. When the citizens of Babel started to build their idolatrous tower to make a name for themselves, God resolved to intervene to stop them: "Come, let us go down and there confuse their language, so that they may not understand one another's speech" (Gen. 11:7, ESV).

And when, following the death of Judah's king Uzziah, God looked for someone to act as his mouthpiece for the next phase of prophetic ministry, Isaiah recalled, "I heard the voice of the Lord saying, 'Whom shall I send? And who will go for us?'" (Isaiah 6:8).

Again, God speaks of himself in the plural. His oneness is not undifferentiated. He is not a mere singularity.

This plurality helps us start to make sense of something else we see in the Old Testament. On several occasions something is identified with God while also being shown as distinct from him. Let's look at a couple of quick examples.

The angel of God

It's the middle of another hot day. Abraham is sitting at the entrance to his tent. It's nap time, but God has other plans. He decides to visit Abraham. "The LORD appeared to Abraham near the great trees of Mamre while he was sitting at the entrance to his tent in the heat of the day. Abraham looked up and saw three men standing nearby" (Gen. 18:1–2).

The writer of Genesis tells us that "The LORD appeared to Abraham," but all Abraham sees as he looks up is that three

guys have shown up. He springs into action and is the con-
summate host, bowing low in respect and tending their every
need: water for their feet, shade and a seat for some rest, and a
copious meal. Actually he treats them royally, all the while
apparently unaware that it is God who has come to lunch.

As time goes on, the true identity of the visitors becomes
apparent. As they address Abraham and Sarah we are told that
it is "the LORD" who spoke. Later, as Abraham walks with
the three men, God again speaks to him, and at the end of the
conversation two of the men head off while Abraham remains
with God. The next we hear of these two men is when we are
told, "The two angels arrived at Sodom" (Gen. 19:1).

The boundaries seem somewhat blurred: men/angels/
God. There is complexity here, and it continues. When Jacob
wrestled with the angel of God, he could say at the end of it
that he had actually been wrestling with God himself: "I have
seen God face to face" (Gen. 32:30, ESV).

But it all makes sense in the light of what we have already
seen: there is a plurality to God. He is not one person, but
three. Accounts of "the angel of the Lord" reflect this. *Angel*
simply means "messenger." Ordinarily this refers to created
spiritual beings, such as those who startled the shepherds by
turning up en masse to announce the birth of Jesus. But when
an angel is spoken of in divine terms, it cannot be a created
angelic being; it can mean only that God himself has come to
bring a message directly to his people. A messenger of God
who is himself divine makes sense only if God is more than
one person.

The Christ of God

This same way of speaking—distinct from God while also
being in some way identified with him—is used of the king
that God promises his people in the Old Testament.

In Isaiah 9, a child is promised to be born to God's people—a child who will grow to rule an ever-expanding and eternal kingdom. His titles will include "Wonderful Counsellor, Mighty God, Everlasting Father, Prince of Peace" (Isa. 9:6). It's a passage that is very familiar. I have Handel playing in my head right now. But we mustn't let our familiarity with it dull its extraordinary message. This *child* to be born will be called *God*. He is not only sent *from* God but also addressed *as* God.

Or consider another well-known Old Testament promise, this time from Daniel.

> In my vision at night I looked, and there before me was one like a son of man, coming with the clouds of heaven. He approached the Ancient of Days and was led into his presence. He was given authority, glory and sovereign power; all peoples, nations and men of every language worshipped him. His dominion is an everlasting dominion that will not pass away, and his kingdom is one that will never be destroyed. (Dan. 7:13–14)

Here we see an ultimate coronation. This figure is presented to God and receives a kingdom that is universal (all peoples, nations, and languages) and eternal ("an everlasting dominion"). Again, a human figure at the head of a divine kingdom.

Psalm 45 is a wedding song, and while the bride makes an appearance, the main focus is on the groom. For while the bride has much to commend her, the groom is (so to speak) out of this world.

> In your majesty ride forth victoriously
>> on behalf of truth, humility and righteousness;
>> let your right hand display awesome deeds.

Let your sharp arrows pierce the hearts of the king's enemies;
    let the nations fall beneath your feet.
Your throne, O God, will last for ever and ever;
    a sceptre of justice will be the sceptre of your kingdom.
You love righteousness and hate wickedness;
      therefore God, your God, has set you above your
         companions
      by anointing you with the oil of joy. (Ps. 45:4–7)

This groom is majestic. In fact, he is divine, addressed by the psalmist as no less than "God." But notice too that this divine groom is anointed by *his* God. He is both God and distinct from God. Assuming that the psalmist doesn't have blurred vision, this is again hugely significant. He is one God. But here we see two persons who are each fully divine.

These examples—the plurality, angel, and Christ of God—are very significant. They all reflect that God is more than one person. Indeed, these texts will make little sense otherwise. God's oneness is affirmed in the Old Testament alongside the fact that he is plural in personhood.

That the Old Testament is clear on this from its earliest pages shows that God did not begin dealing with his people as a singular person and then somehow progressively become more trinitarian as time went on. Nor was it the case that the Father related directly to people in the Old Testament and only in the New required his Son to act as go-between, as though the Father suddenly needed a PA for everyone to go through. God has always been three persons, and that is reflected throughout the Scriptures.

What *does* change, however, as we move into the New Testament is that the theological framework that makes sense of all this is made more explicit.

GOD AS TRINITY IN THE NEW TESTAMENT

Most of the lights in the main living area of my house are operated by dimmer switches. When the light is dimmed way down and the room is almost dark, it is possible to see the main furniture only in outline. You can really only make out the shapes of the sofas and tables. Slowly turn up the lights and gradually the details become filled in—the outlines take on a fuller texture and color, becoming defined and clearly visible.

The revelation of God in the Bible is cumulative. The light of his self-disclosure gradually increases as he reveals more and more of himself and as he expands his promises to his people. The effect is similar to turning up the dimmer switch. As God the Son becomes flesh and enters our world, the revelation reaches its fullest brightness. What was suggestive of God's triune nature in the Old Testament is made explicit in the New. What was perceived in outlines can now be seen in much greater clarity: God is triune. As Jesus himself has told us, the name of God is the name of "the Father and of the Son and of the Holy Spirit."

We see this in what the New Testament shows us about both Jesus and the Holy Spirit.

The humanity of Jesus

The gospel accounts of Jesus' life make it very clear that he was as fully human as you and I. Jesus was not like Superman when he's in Clark Kent mode, *pretending* to need glasses or get hurt or struggle lifting something heavy. His humanity was not affected but real.

He had a human body. He was born as a child and needed to grow and develop physically. He needed to grow in strength. His body was subject to the same limitations and vulner-abilities of any body. Jesus got tired and hungry and thirsty.[4]

When at the end of his life he was flogged and beaten, he was weakened so severely that someone else had to carry his cross.[5] His body bruised, his body hurt, and, in the end, his body died.

Jesus had a human mind. He grew in wisdom. There were times when he needed to ask things. He had human emotions. He was not aloof and detached from what was going on around him. In the Gospels we see him going through the whole range of emotions: joy, sorrow, love, compassion, astonishment, and anger. At times his emotions were intense. He felt deep anxiety and distress. He wept at the graveside of Lazarus. He felt overwhelming sorrow.[6] He was not emotionally impervious to the things going on around him.

In all this we see that Jesus was authentically human. Contrary to how Jesus has been depicted in stained glass and Christian art, he did not walk around in a woman's nightgown or look like one of the Bee Gees. He would have looked how any regular guy at that time would have looked.

The divinity of Jesus

The Gospels are equally clear that Jesus was fully divine. The pattern we have seen in the Old Testament of someone being simultaneously described as distinct from God and identified with him reaches its climax in the New Testament's teaching about who Jesus is: "In the beginning was the Word, and the Word was with God, and the Word was God" (John 1:1). *With* God. *Was* God. Distinct from God and yet also addressed as God.

He claimed as much repeatedly. On one occasion Jesus was teaching in a very crowded home. During the course of his teaching, bits of dust and stone began to drop down from above and it quickly became apparent that a group of men on the flat roof were trying to burrow their way through. As sunlight broke through and a sizeable hole appeared, another figure emerged, silhouetted against the light and on a stretcher of some kind. As his friends began awkwardly to lower him down, some of the crowd stepped back and allowed him to come down to the ground in front of Jesus. No doubt the room would have fallen silent and the teaching ground to a halt. Remains of the ceiling would have been everywhere. The man was paralyzed. Everyone's gaze switched from him to Jesus, waiting to see what would happen next.

What did happen next surprised everyone. "[Jesus] said to the paralytic, 'My son, your sins are forgiven'" (Mark 2:5).

The surprise for many came from the fact that sins didn't seem to be this man's issue. He was paralyzed. His friends had gone to considerable length to bring him to Jesus. Someone was going to have to have a lengthy and difficult conversation with their home insurers. This man's need was obvious. And Jesus was a healer. The man wanted to be able to walk and run and jump and dance. He didn't want four guys carrying him around. But Jesus starts talking about his sin.

If they were surprised because Jesus seemed to be missing the point, others in the room were shocked for a very different reason: "Some teachers of the law were sitting there, thinking to themselves, 'Why does this fellow talk like that? He's blaspheming! Who can forgive sins but God alone?'" (Mark 2:6–7). They had caught on to something important. It was God's right—and his alone—to forgive sin.

Imagine I met you one day, threw a punch at you, and knocked you out. And imagine that while you lay there, a passerby came up to me and said, "Sam, it's okay. I forgive you." When eventually you regained consciousness (just to warn you, it could be days), you would not be impressed at this person extending me forgiveness. *You* are the injured party. It is only you who can offer forgiveness.

When it comes to human sins, God is always the injured party. Whomever else the sin may affect, it is ultimately a sin against God himself. It is for him to forgive.

What Jesus is claiming here is astounding. All sin everywhere, Jesus says, is a sin against him personally. Every sin this paralyzed man had ever committed—every unkind act, improper word, and illicit thought—all came down to this: they were for Jesus to forgive. A sin against God is a sin against Jesus. The point was not lost on the scribes. Jesus was claiming to be God.

This is just one example of many. Jesus claimed to be that divine figure promised in the Old Testament—the Son of Man.[7] He took onto himself, without embarrassment, the personal name God had revealed to his people. He claimed to have existed before Abraham and been the fulfilment of that great man's faith.[8] He claimed to be one with God the Father.[9] Such claims were not ambiguous to those who first heard them in Jesus' day. They accused him of blasphemy. They reached for the nearest stone to throw at him.

But it wasn't just his claims; Jesus also performed amazing deeds—deeds which can really be understood only in the light of his full divinity. He walked on water, healed the sick, drove out demons, and even sent a severe storm packing just by *speaking* to it (ever tried that?). And he raised the dead. People hadn't realized before Jesus that a funeral could be unsuccessful. But above all, Jesus let people worship him as divine. When Thomas acclaimed Jesus to be "My Lord and my God!" (John 20:28), the one thing Jesus didn't do was put him in a straightjacket and find him the nearest padded room.

Thomas had realized, and Jesus had confirmed, that the one true God was present before him in human form.

The divinity of the Spirit

We also see in the New Testament a clear sense of the Holy Spirit's being both divine and also a distinct person.

The divinity of the Spirit is assumed in the New Testament. The opening words of the Bible describe the Spirit as the "Spirit of God." The Spirit is the divine agency through which God works, and the work of the Spirit is the work of God. The presence of the Spirit is the presence of God. When King David pleads with God not to remove the Spirit from him, he is pleading not to have the very presence of God taken from him.

In the New Testament, the Holy Spirit is equated with God in an almost casual manner. How you treat the Spirit is how you treat God. So when Peter exposes the deceit of Ananias, he can accuse him in one moment of lying "to the Holy Spirit" and then in the next of lying "to God."[10] The two are equivalent. By lying to the Spirit you are lying to God because the Spirit is in every way God.

The personhood of the Spirit

The New Testament also shows the Spirit as being personal. It is easy for Christians to think of the Spirit as though he were some abstract force used by God from time to time—a cross between a cattle-prod and gasoline. And so we can often speak of the Spirit in ways that are impersonal: a divine force that convicts or awakens or equips. But we need to remember that the Spirit is a person. Jesus speaks of the Spirit as a "he," not an "it." He is every bit as much a person as the Father and the Son. In the Bible, we see the Spirit's work described in personal terms: he persuades, prays, testifies, cries out, creates, judges, leads, has a mind, can be blasphemed, and can be grieved. The Holy Spirit is not just raw divine power that sloshes around inside of us; he is a person who indwells us and to whom we can relate.

WHAT THE TRINITY IS AND ISN'T

And so we return to the verse with which we started, Jesus calling on his followers to make new disciples: "Baptising them in the name of the Father and of the Son and of the Holy Spirit" (Matt. 28:19).

This pretty much wraps it up for us. There is one God; he is three persons. To clarify what's being said, it's helpful to look at what's not being said.

Not three gods

Jesus is not saying there are three gods (an idea called tritheism). This is unfortunately the caricature that some people have of Christianity—that we believe in a trio of separate deities. But there is one name, not three. Jesus did not say, "in the *names* [plural] of the Father and of the Son and of the Holy Spirit," as if there were three completely separate gods. He said, "in the *name* [singular] of the Father and of the Son and of the Holy Spirit."

There was no little committee of gods who put their heads together to come up with this universe. Jesus speaks of the one name—the singular name—of God because there is one God and not three.

Not three aspects

Nor does the Trinity describe three aspects of God. This is a belief (called modalism) which says that the Trinity describes three separate roles that the one God plays. He is the Father at one point, then the Son at another point, and then the

Spirit at another, like someone playing multiple roles. The effect is that God ends up being like Robin Williams's character in the comedy *Mrs. Doubtfire,* in which a separated dad masquerades as the kids' nanny so that he can spend more time with them. In one scene he is in "dad mode," in another he is in "nanny mode," dressed as a little old lady and affecting a Scottish accent. It is a classic farce, as circumstances overtake him and he is forced to switch between his different personae.

This is not what we are dealing with here. Jesus did not say, "in the name of the *Father, Son, and Spirit,*" as though they were merely roles God slips into and out of. He said, "in the name of the Father *and of* the Son *and of* the Holy Spirit," emphasizing the fact that the one name of God belongs fully to each distinct person.

Not a contradiction

Nor is it a contradiction to speak of God in this way. One God, three persons. Some will say that this doesn't and can't make sense. If they are Christians they might allow for it by making recourse to the fact that it is all a "mystery," and so there is no real need to think about it. If they are not Christians, then it may just confirm their suspicions that Christianity is fundamentally irrational and doesn't need to be bothered with.

But there is no contradiction here. The way in which God is one is different from the way in which he is three. As Fred Sanders puts it, "God is not one something and also somehow three of the same somethings."[11] If we were to say, "God is one person and God is three persons," this would be a contradiction. But the way in which he is one is not the same as the way in which he is three. He is one in name and nature and he is three in person. This may be—okay, *is*—hard for us to understand, but at the very least we need to recognize that it is not contradictory. The center of our faith, that which stands behind all of reality, is not an enormous, cosmic contradiction.

The name into which we Christians are baptized—the name of God—shows us that God is triune. This is not something he becomes as Scripture unfolds; it is who he is and always has been. God is one. And that one God is three persons.

4

THE PARTY THAT NEVER ENDS

God as Trinity: Part 2

I'M A BIT OF a sucker for the bonus features on DVDs. Often I'll skip past the main movie and dive straight into the "Making of" segments. Usually it is a somewhat disappointing experience—just some promotional interviews with the main cast and crew gushing about how, like, *amazing* it was working together on this movie and how Cruise is such a regular guy in person.

But every now and then you strike gold. You get beyond the plastic interviews and instead get some of what really goes on behind the scenes. You'll have the director talking you through some of the trickier decisions made on set or explaining why a particular scene was done in a particular way. I find it all fascinating. In the best cases, it makes sense of how it all works as a movie.

One of the thrills of looking at the doctrine of the Trinity is that we get something of a peek behind the scenes on the inner workings of God. And, like the best DVD featurette, it can have the effect of giving us a deeper appreciation of all that has been done for us. It makes sense of the way God is and how he works.

Jesus gives us a window into how his relationship with the Father works in the following passage:

> Jesus gave them this answer: "I tell you the truth, the Son can do nothing by himself; he can do only what he sees his Father doing, because whatever the Father does the Son also does. For the Father loves the Son and shows him all he does. Yes, to your amazement he will show him even greater things than these. For just as the Father raises the dead and gives them life, even so the Son gives life to whom he is pleased to give it. Moreover, the Father judges no-one, but has entrusted all judgment to the Son, that all may honour the Son just as they honour the Father. He who does not honour the Son does not honour the Father, who sent him." (John 5:19–23)

This is an amazing insight into the relationships of the Trinity—the dynamic that really exists within the Godhead.

IDENTIFICATION BETWEEN FATHER AND SON

Jesus tells us that whatever the Father does, the Son does. Jesus has just performed a miracle on the Sabbath, healing a disabled man. Some of the Jews took issue with this, claiming such an act to be unlawful on the Sabbath. Jesus responds to them by making an astonishing claim: "My Father is always at his work to this very day, and I, too, am working" (John 5:17).

Jesus is making a strong connection between the work of God the Father, which is ongoing, and the work he himself is doing. His act of healing the man is bound up with the very work of God. This is a connection that draws an even more hostile response from his opponents: "For this reason the Jews tried all the harder to kill him; not only was he breaking the Sabbath, but he was even calling God his own Father, making himself equal with God" (John 5:18).

Jesus is claiming divine warrant for what he has been doing, and he does so on the basis that he is the Son of God. As he expands on this, he demonstrates that, as the Son, all he does is a reflection of what the Father does. None of it is independent of the Father or by the Son's exclusive initiative. It has all been shown to him by the Father.

This is a concept we can understand but that probably doesn't resonate with us today in the way it would have with its original readers. In Jesus' day, you would have done what your father did. It would have been the family trade. If your father was a fisherman, you followed in his footsteps and worked with him as a fisherman. If he was a carpenter, you were a carpenter. If he was a tanner, you were a tanner.

This is obviously not so today. You do not inevitably go into your father's trade. His vocation is not necessarily yours, and few of us now even get to see our fathers in their workplace.

But in Jesus' day, that was the way it worked. What your father did, you did. His trade was your trade. And Jesus is saying that is also true of his own "spiritual trade." He does what he does for the simple reason that it is what God the Father does. Why did he heal on the Sabbath? Because it is part of the family business. Whatever the Father does, the Son does. Their work is of a piece.

Yet the identification between Father and Son is far more than vocational. It is familial: "For the Father loves the Son and shows him all he does" (John 5:20). And the Father showing the Son everything he does, so that the Son will follow, is not born out of economic necessity (as it would have been for people at that time). Rather, it is an expression of the Father's delight in the Son. The Father loves showing the Son his work because he loves his Son. It is the Father's joy to share his work with the Son.

And healing an invalid is just the start of it. The Father's most glorious work is yet to come:

> For the Father loves the Son and shows him all he does. Yes, to your amazement he will show him even greater things than these. For just as the Father raises the dead and gives them life, even so the Son gives life to whom he is pleased to give it. (John 5:20–21)

One of the key works of the Father is giving life to the dead. This is something that defines who God is: raising the dead and giving them life. The history of God's people was peppered with instances that reflected this. God's stock-in-trade is bringing life from non-life. And now we see that he shares this with the Son. The Son himself is authorized by the Father to impart life to whoever he chooses.

The conclusion of all this comes in the final parallelism:

> Moreover, the Father judges no-one, but has entrusted all judgment to the Son, that all may honour the Son just as they honour the Father. He who does not honour the Son does not honour the Father, who sent him. (John 5:22–23)

Just as the Father is to be honored, so too is the Son. So closely are Father and Son identified that failure to honor the Son is failure to honor the Father whose work he shares and whose love he receives.

So we can see an unmistakable "closeness" between Father and Son. But we mustn't equate their identification with each other as being identical to each other. There is identification but also distinction. The Father is the Father and the Son is the Son. They are different, and the dynamic between them also reflects this.

DISTINCTION BETWEEN FATHER AND SON

Intrinsic to this dynamic is the fact that it is the Father's place to show and the Son's place to see and to follow. The Father shows the Son his work, but the Son doesn't show the Father. The Son can do nothing by himself, but the same is not true of the Father.

This is seen in the divine prerogative of judgment: "Moreover, the Father judges no-one, but has entrusted all judgment to the Son" (John 5:22). All judgment has been entrusted by the Father to the Son. The Father now judges no-one; this is the Son's sole responsibility. But notice that it is the Father who does the entrusting. The solemn task of judgment is his to allocate. It is not the Son's by right; it has been granted to him by the Father. The Father entrusts; the Son receives.

The dynamic between them has a particular shape, one in which it is the Father's prerogative to do and initiate certain things and the Son's to follow and receive. The Father and the Son are closely identified with each other, but clearly not identical.

Two important facts flow from this.

The Trinity is not just how God is to us, but how he is in himself

The Trinity is not just God's public face. It is how he is "at home."

Some families have very different public and private faces.

Behind closed doors on their own there is a dynamic that's different from when others are around. On their own they are fractious and openly insulting to one another, but in company all is sweetness and light. Most of us, in fact, moderate our home life when in the presence of others. But in some cases the public and private demeanors can be very different indeed. Think of a Hollywood couple who make a very public (and expensive) effort to insist that their marriage is going great and that they are still fantastically in love. And yet, it eventually comes out that there has been a string of infidelities and it's all been coming apart at the seams.

There is nothing of this public/private mismatch with God. The Trinity is not just a front that God puts on when we are around. It's who he really is in himself. It is not his "professional" behavior or a convenient way of presenting himself to us in our limited understanding. To himself, the one God is three distinct persons. What he allows us to see is in fact the reality of who he really is.

Father, Son, and Spirit are not temporary roles, but eternal identities

God has always been triune—three persons. And those persons have always been Father, Son, and Holy Spirit. They have existed eternally in those roles. It was not that God had been triune and then, when it came to providing salvation for humanity, the three persons had to work out who would do what. There was no pre-creation drawing of straws to determine which person would have which role in the economy of the gospel—who would do the Father/initiating stuff and who would do the Son/responding stuff, like schoolkids deciding who is going to be "it" at the start of a game of tag. It was not that one of them called shotgun on being the Father, leaving the other two to figure out between them who would get to be the Spirit and who would have to go into the world to die for sin.

As we have seen from John 5, there is a particular shape to how the persons of the Trinity relate to one another. That shape has always existed, and the dynamic has always been there. We'll see more of this in due course, but for now we're going to focus on one of the most famous verses in the Bible: "For God so loved the world that he gave his one and only Son, that whoever believes in him shall not perish but have eternal life" (John 3:16).

The Father sends. The Son is being sent. Before Jesus was born, the Son existed as the Son. It was not a role he assumed for the first time that first Christmas. For the Father to have sent the Son, there had to have always been a Father and a Son. God is triune; he has always been triune; and the persons of the Trinity have always been Father, Son, and Holy Spirit.

WHY THIS MATTERS AND WHAT THE TRINITY SHOWS

It always matters to understand the truths God has revealed to us about himself, because their purpose is that we can know him. God wants us to understand what he has shown us of his nature, and it is a great blessing for us to do so. Even when this involves considerable mental effort, as it surely does with the Trinity, it is an effort well worth expending. Friends of mine who fanatically follow soccer never considered learning the off-side rule an unnecessary hassle. Understanding it gives them a greater capacity to engage with the game and appreciate all that is happening on the field.

As we grasp what it means for God to be triune we are better able to appreciate who he is and how he has been at work in this world.

God is eternally loving and just

God is Trinity. He is community. He has always been so. There was never a time when the Trinity was not in relationship. And the relationships of the Trinity have always been perfect. God has always possessed the traits that make for the very best relationships: love, faithfulness, honesty, righteousness. This is significant because these qualities cannot exist except in relationship.

Love exists only where there is more than one person. If God were only a singularity, a solitary person existing alone for eternity, then love is not something he could have experienced or exhibited before creation. Love would not be part of his eternal nature, just something he started making a stab at once he'd created beings to love. But because he is triune, we can say that love has existed within God for all eternity. It is part of his unchanging, eternal nature. C. S. Lewis puts it this way: "The words 'God is love' have no real meaning unless God contains at least two persons. Love is something one person has for another person. If God was a single person, then before the world was made, he was not love."[1]

The reality of the Trinity shows us not just that "God can love," or even that "God has loved," but that "God is love." It is not a temporal characteristic but an eternal one. It is not just a phase he is going through and might come out of. It is not just something he sometimes does; it is who he is. God has always been love, for he has always been Trinity.

The same is true of other relational qualities also. Think of righteousness and justice. These too depend on the presence of relationship; they describe the actions of one person in relation to another. Neither can exist outside of relationship. But since the persons of the Trinity have always been in relationship, we can say that these, too, belong to God's eternal character. He has always been righteous and he has always been just, for he has always been triune. Just as we can truly say that "God is love," so too we can truly say that "God is justice."

Such comments could not be made about a non-trinitarian. However loving such a God might be to his people, we could never say that love was intrinsic to his being. It would not be part of his unchanging and eternal character. There could be no ultimate confidence before such a God, no basis on which to know how he might act.

God is not dependent on us

God did not make us in order to fulfill some unmet relational need within him. The Trinity is already perfect community. The persons of the Godhead take unending delight in one another. God was not bored or lacking in some way. He didn't spend eternity before creation in loneliness wondering when it would be time to create some company. Because God is triune, he has never been solitary. The persons of the Trinity have always enjoyed a perfect life with one another.

The persons of the Trinity have always enjoyed a perfect life with one another.

It can be a strange moment when a child realizes for the first time that, once upon a time, his or her parents had a life of their own as a couple before having children. I can remember it slowly dawning on me as I grew up that my parents had enjoyed a period of time together before my brother and I came along. They had lived for a while in Australia before returning to the UK and settling down. I can remember them showing us photo albums from this time and telling us stories about various things that had happened. They had had a happy time together quite apart from us.

This had never really occurred to me before. I think I must have assumed that life for my parents had started when we children turned up. But there they were in a far-off land, enjoying a life of their own. They were not simply on board as co-parents but had a relationship together all of their own.

Realizing that you are not the center of it all actually leads to greater security. Being at the center involves carrying the huge burden of knowing that everything ultimately comes down to you. Rather than being the *cause* of your parents' happiness, you can begin to see yourself instead as the *product* of your parents' happiness. It does not all depend on you. Something else is at the heart of it.

We undergo a similar shift in thinking as we begin to grasp the significance of the Trinity. God did not make us because he needed us. He was in no way relationally deficient without us. We were not created to satisfy some craving within him. He was not friendless and lonely.

This can be an unsettling thing to realize. We may have thought in our early Christian days that God's plans and affections were all about us. We were at the center of God's heart. But then we begin to glimpse the sheer delight that the persons of the Trinity have for one another. And we start to realize that within the Trinity God had a life of his own that was quite apart from us. He had been utterly complete in himself before we entered into the frame. We begin to see ourselves not primarily as the cause of our God's happiness, but as the product of it.

As with the child, this is the way to a deeper security. We are not the complete center of God's world. He is. The Trinity shows us our true place, not at the center but in orbit around it. Rather than thinking we're the point of it all, we get to enjoy what really is the point of it all: God's enjoyment of himself as Trinity.

The true goal of the gospel

By the time it reached its finale in 2004, *Friends* was the most successful sitcom in US television history. It lasted ten years and ran for 236 episodes. At the height of its popularity its six main stars were each earning $1 million per episode. It was huge.

Its success arguably stemmed from the relationships between those six main characters. It was the set of friendships that was deeply attractive. We felt as though we knew them; we *liked* them. Here was an attractive little community. We wanted to join in.

This was no accident. Part of the thinking behind the show was to create a gang you would want to be part of. At one stage in its development it was going to be called *Friends Like Us*, but then its makers realized that this sounded exclusive and so it became just *Friends*. It was open-ended. There was room for others to join.

The gospel is sometimes spoken of as if it were just a meal ticket to a better life in heaven. Sometimes it's described as little more than a means of forgiveness and the avoidance of punishment. But ultimately it's an invitation to come into the fellowship of the Trinity. Through the death and resurrection of Christ, this perfect set of relationships has been opened out for us to join. Again, Fred Sanders hits the nail on the head:

> This is what the doctrine of the Trinity helps us learn with greater precision: that God is love. The triune God is a love that is infinitely high above you, eternally preceding you, and welcoming you in.
>
> God the Father sent the Son to do something for us and the Spirit to be something in us, to bring us into the family life of God.[2]

The death and resurrection of Jesus means that we can be part of the relationships of the Trinity. This perfect matrix of love, which has existed at the center of all reality for all eternity, is open for us to join. Through the gospel, we have been invited in. Amazing!

PART 2
THE TRINITY AND US

5

YOU: AN INTRODUCTION[1]
The Trinity and Humanity

THERE ARE SEVERAL WAYS to spot someone who's spent a year abroad:

1. They wear beads.
2. They insist on affecting the local accent when pronouncing the names of the places they've visited. This is to underline just how truly they have assimilated all the cultural conventions.
3. They have an incredible ability to turn any aspect of any conversation on any subject to something they did or saw during their year abroad—a knack of conversational dexterity that would provoke the most accomplished evangelist to envy. (This was me when I got back from my gap year in Kenya—or "Keenya" as I would have said it—and I would like to take this opportunity to apologize right now to anyone who knew me in 1994.)
4. They have *found themselves.*

This last point, it seems, is pretty much the purpose of it all. Learning how to find ourselves has become a fixation of the last decade or so. It has become a growing industry. A moment or two of cursory research on the Internet indicates that adults can find themselves in any number of ways—playing with Legos and coloring were two that immediately caught my eye. But the favored method seems to be going off and traveling somewhere. Preferably exotic. (I have yet to meet someone who found themselves in Cleveland.)

Yet for all the fun I want to poke at it, talk of finding yourself is actually a reflection of something significant. It expresses something most of us experience in one way or another and resonates with something the Bible has testified to all along: we are easily confused about who we are.

The Bible accounts for this in a way that is straightforward to understand, but very hard to truly accept. All of us have become skewed versions of who we were made to be. There is a sense in which we no longer (or, rather, can't) relate rightly to ourselves. There was a point, long ago, when the bridges of self-understanding were burned down. We are left with a sense—profound in some, slight in others—of self-alienation. And so we look in all sorts of wacky places for the answer. Except in the one place that actually has it.

A while ago I was struck by an interesting notion (to me, in any case). We live in a universe and on a planet created by God. We ourselves have not only been created by this God but also uniquely bear his stamp, his likeness, in a way that no other creature does. We do not bear it consistently, but we do bear it truly. We have been made in his image.

So here's the notion: whatever we learn about this God is going to have a practical benefit to how we understand the universe in which we live and—more pressingly—ourselves.

God made us to "image" him; the more we understand him, the better we will understand who he has made us to be. Understanding God can be hard work, but the payoff is enormous. A small insight into God can yield a huge insight into ourselves. So when we begin to grasp that God is triune, we can expect it to have some important practical application to our lives.

Genesis 1: The creation of the world. God speaks. Stuff appears. There was evening; there was morning. Repeat.

The biblical account of creation in Genesis 1 is formulaic and intentionally so. It is showing us not just that reality is created, but that its creation was orderly. There is nothing arbitrary or haphazard about the process. Nothing is flung together. It is organized, crafted, and meticulous.

A small insight into God can yield a huge insight into ourselves.

For much of the creation account, God creates by issuing instructions. Whether he is forming land or seas or sky or is filling them with things, there is a similar kind of approach: "Let there be . . ." or "Let the land produce . . ." God is summoning. It is as if there is a vast army of underlings rushing about executing every utterance. Except there isn't— God creates through his word. Put another way, his word is so powerful that it effects the very thing it announces. God doesn't issue a declaration and then stand back while the little people put it all in place. He says it, and it is. That's how powerful his word is.

But the pattern changes when it comes to the creating of people. We would expect God to say something like "Let the ground produce people" or "May there be men and women around the place." But instead he says, "Let us make . . ." We have already seen that this formulation reflects something of the plural nature of God. But it does something else too. It draws attention to this particular act of creation.

Why is it introduced differently?

"Let us make." It is as if for this particular bit God is rolling up his sleeves and getting especially involved. The formula is different because what he is making is different. What is about to come off the production line is unlike anything that has come before. We're about to see something unique in all creation.

IN THE IMAGE OF GOD

Humans are special. Even before we appear, we are given special billing. We matter to God in a way that a stag beetle or dolphin doesn't. And we're not left guessing as to what it is that sets us apart. God tells us.

It's not just that we come with some features other animals lack (such as opposable thumbs). We are made in God's likeness. Okay, so all of creation reflects something of its maker. We're told, for example, that "the heavens declare the glory of God" (Ps. 19:1). Paul tells us that something of God's divine power and glory is seen in creation (Rom. 1:20). But our capacity to reflect something of God is unique. There is a correspondence between us and God that exists nowhere else. Wayne Grudem reminds us that every human person we encounter is "a creature of God who is *more like God than anything else in the universe.*"[2] Whatever marvels we end up discovering between our suburb of the Milky Way and the outer reaches of the universe will not compare in wonder to humanity. Our sin has marred this image, but it still remains. Like the reflection in a cracked and fading mirror, the likeness—though distorted and dim—nevertheless remains. However much we have turned from God and departed from his vocation for us, we retain the dignity of reflecting something of him to the rest of creation.

I need to remember this. I live in a crowded part of the world. People are everywhere. Too many of them are normally driving on the same road as me. It's easy for me to see them as little more than impediments to a quick journey home, as things to be overtaken. How wrong I am. When someone next cuts me off, my reflex should not be to imagine how convenient it would be for their car to instantly combust, but to remember that they are someone who bears the image of God. (As well as being a bad driver.)

RELATIONSHIPS MATTER

The account of our creation in Genesis goes on to show us something of what this involves. In fact, we have already been given a pretty big hint. "Then God said, 'Let us make man in our image, in our likeness'" (Gen. 1:26).

As we have seen, in this verse God highlights his plurality, his "us"-ness. And he does so just as he comes to create a creature in his image. This is not an accident of timing. It shows us what it means to be made in his likeness. The God in whose image we are made is triune, three persons in relationship. Likewise we have been designed for relationship, to be in community. It does not exhaust all it means to be made in God's image, but it is one of the most important aspects of it. Intrinsic to our humanness is that we are relational.

This sheds light on a number of important areas. We are not just human creatures; we are persons. And a person is set apart and defined by his relationship to other persons. Here's Tim Chester: "The doctrine of the Trinity shows us that relationships are essential for personhood. A 'person' is like a 'mother' or a 'son.' It has no meaning apart from relationships with other people. You cannot be a childless mother, a parentless son or a relationless person."[3]

We sense this. For some of us it is screamingly obvious. A golfing friend of mine says that one of the worst experiences of his golfing life was getting a hole in one while playing on his own. A spectacular shot, but no one to see it. Great experiences are often greater when they are shared, dark experiences often darker when they are not. One of the ways in which we punish someone as a society is by removing him from it. The most severe punishment can be solitary confinement. That this is an extreme punishment reflects how deeply we sense that relationship is intrinsic to our humanness. To choose to live in virtual isolation would not seem natural to us. It contradicts one of the most basic purposes for which we were made. It undermines our humanity to be away from community.

We are not just human creatures; we are persons.

Stuff first; people second

This speaks powerfully into Western culture. Many of us have been taken in by the appeal of materialism: putting "stuff" before people. But to elevate the acquisition of ever more material things above cultivating deep, healthy community is dehumanizing. Stuff is not designed to fulfill our humanity; but relationships are—relationships with others and with God himself.

This is powerfully illustrated by the George Clooney movie *Up in the Air*. Clooney plays Ryan Bingham, a business executive hired by firms to lay off their staff for them. Most of his time is spent in the supposed happy solitude of travel, in the world of exclusive airline lounges and reward schemes. "To know me is to fly with me. This is where I live. It's these kinds of systematized friendly touches that keep my world in orbit."[4]

On the side he does motivational speaking, in which he commends this philosophy to others. His pitch revolves around the notion that the less relational baggage we carry the quicker we will get on in life. Here's Bingham in full swing:

> What's in your backpack? How much does your life weigh? We weigh ourselves down until we can't move. And make no mistake: moving is living.
>
> You have a new backpack, only this time I want you to fill it with people. Feel the weight of that bag. Make no mistake, your relationships are the heaviest components in your life. You feel the straps cutting into your shoulders. All those negotiations and arguments and secrets and compromises. You don't need to carry all that weight. Why don't you set that bag down?
>
> Some animals were meant to carry each other, to live symbiotically for a lifetime. Star-crossed lovers, monogamous swans. We are not those animals. The slower we move, the faster we die. We are not swans. We're sharks.[5]

It sounds compelling. He seems to embody the success of this philosophy. He has carved out a life for himself largely free of emotional commitments. He hardly sees his family and has a casual attitude to friendship and sexual relationships. Success for him is measured in the accumulation of air miles. He prefers the "synthetic courtesy" of his top-tier loyalty programs to anything else.

Yet it all strikes a hollow note. As the movie develops we become increasingly aware of what, in fact, Bingham is missing out on.

It is a commentary on what we have seen in Genesis 1. To look for fulfillment outside of having true relationships is ultimately dehumanizing. And yet this reflects the attitude of many today. We define ourselves by what we have rather than by who we are in relationship with others. We sacrifice friendship, marriage, parenting, service to others, on the altar of material gain. And when that doesn't seem to fulfill us, we assume it is because we have not gained enough. And so we push to acquire more and more. It is a vicious circle that takes us further and further away from who we were made and meant to be.

The Bible is not against prosperity. It is not necessarily a sin to have considerable wealth. But it is not the goal for which we were made.

SERVICE MATTERS

A few years ago I spent a summer working for a church in downtown Bangkok. It was an incredible experience in all sorts of ways. I had never seen a church with such staggering diversity. There were refugees on the edge of poverty shoulder to shoulder with executives from leading global companies. Lurching from one world to the other was something I never quite got used to.

On one occasion a family invited me to stay with them for a couple of nights to get a good break from my ministry. I soon discovered that they were very wealthy indeed. The first sign of this was that they sent a car to pick me up. But the real eye-popping moment came when we drove through the gates to their home. As I emerged from the car, security guards clicked their heels to attention and saluted me. This was something I could get used to!

It was a remarkable home. I had a number of rooms put at my disposal. Unseen domestic staff seemed to lurk everywhere. It seemed that any time my back was turned for more than a moment, I would look around to discover that the cushions had been mysteriously fluffed up and my belongings straightened. It was like having a cross between a housemaid and a ninja.

But the real highlight came when my hosts needed to run out. They thrust a card into my hand with a menu and the number of their chef. I was to call any time I was hungry and tell him what I wanted, and he would cook it and someone would come knocking on the door moments later with my meal. I could *definitely* get used to this.

My host, it transpired, ran the Asia division of a large multi-national. He was a very powerful man, as was apparent within moments of arriving at his house.

How we do power

In our world we measure power by how many people you have serving you. It might be the number of employees under your authority at work or the size of your domestic staff; the number of people whose professional lives revolve around you tells society whether or not you have made it. A fixation of the British press since the end of Tony Blair's premiership has been his growing wealth and the ever-increasing size of his staff. People at your service equals power—the more people, the more power.

It is in this context that we come across what seems to us to be the most paradoxical thing Jesus ever said: "For even the Son of Man did not come to be served, but to serve, and to give his life as a ransom for many" (Mark 10:45).

"Son of Man" was Jesus' favorite designation for himself. In his Aramaic context it was a roundabout way of talking about yourself, similar to today's use of "oneself." But "Son of Man" also had another meaning. Jesus was using it as something of a theological double entendre. Let's look again at this moment in the book of Daniel:

> In my vision at night I looked, and there before me was one like a son of man, coming with the clouds of heaven. He approached the Ancient of Days and was led into his presence. He was given authority, glory and sovereign power; all peoples, nations and men of every language worshipped him. His dominion is an everlasting dominion that will not pass away, and his kingdom is one that will never be destroyed. (Dan. 7:13–14)

Notice the unprecedented power being given by God to this figure. He is accorded the very authority of God himself. He is to rule on God's behalf over every place for all time. It is an extraordinary coronation.

This colors the way Jesus uses the term "Son of Man." It is a deeply loaded term. Jesus is claiming to be this very figure promised in Daniel's vision. But even more stunning than that is Jesus' insistence that, as the Son of Man, he has come to serve.

How Jesus does power

The implication is clear. If even *he* came to serve—he who is due all earthly authority and power—then how much more should that be true of those who claim to follow him?

It was a much needed point. Immediately before saying these things, Jesus had been prodded by two of his closest disciples for positions of greatness in his forthcoming kingdom. They could see that Jesus was heading for greatness and wanted to call shotgun on the best positions before anyone else did. Once the rest of the disciples caught wind of this they were furious with James and John, presumably because they hadn't thought of it first.

And so Jesus needed to knock their heads together. This way of thinking—power equals greatness—went right against the grain of the kingdom he was about to establish.

> Jesus called them together and said, "You know that those who are regarded as rulers of the Gentiles lord it over them, and their high officials exercise authority over them. Not so with you. Instead, whoever wants to become great among you must be your servant, and whoever wants to be first must be slave of all." (Mark 10:42–44)

Greatness was measured by service. This was to be the radical topography of the new kingdom—the way up is down.

This dynamic was to restore us to the orientation we were created for. We are made for relationship. And the character of the relationships for which we are made is loving relationships, put-the-other-person-first relationships.

Love for others in the Trinity

This, after all, characterizes the relationships of the Trinity, which we are made to reflect. We see in the relationships between the Father, Son, and Spirit a dynamic of love, of other-person-centeredness.[6] We see the Father's deep love for the Son: "The Father loves the Son and has placed everything in his hands" (John 3:35).

We see the Son's deep love for the Father: "The world must learn that I love the Father and that I do exactly what my Father has commanded me" (John 14:31).

And we see the Spirit longing to bring glory to the Son:

But when he, the Spirit of truth, comes, he will guide you into all truth. He will not speak on his own; he will speak only what he hears, and he will tell you what is yet to come. He will bring glory to me by taking from what is mine and making it known to you. (John 16:13–14)

The relationships of the Trinity are relationships of love. They are marked by devotion to the others. The way in which this love is expressed is different in some ways between the different persons, as we shall see later, but whatever differences emerge between how they relate to one another, it all comes within the framework of love.

We often recognize the importance of relationships to a healthy human life. We know we all need them. But we are often less mindful of the character these relationships are meant to exhibit. Relationships for us easily become self serving. We put something into a relationship because of what we can get out of it. We invest in others because of how they make us feel or because of benefits which can come as a result of knowing them. Romantic relationships are often conducted on the basis of "I'll stick with this only as long as I get what I want from it."

But the message of the Trinity is radically different. Self-centeredness poisons the healthy relationships for which we were made. Putting it another way, we are not designed to find happiness in living for ourselves. We were created to enjoy a matrix of relationships in which we can reflect the self-giving relationships of God the Trinity.

MARRIAGE AND SEXUALITY MATTER

Here is another important insight arising from understanding ourselves as made in the image of a trinitarian God. We have already seen that God's oneness is not flat or monochrome. It speaks of his being united within himself, a unity that comes from the perfect integration of the persons of the Godhead, something that is conveyed by that foundational Old Testament creed: "Hear, O Israel: The LORD our God, the LORD is one" (Deut. 6:4).

We find here an interesting parallel between the oneness of God and the relationship between a man and wife.

Adam + Eve = one

Adam has been hard at work in the garden of Eden. At the top of the list has been continuing the work of taxonomy that God began at the beginning of creation. God had named some of the basic elements of the cosmos: day, night, heaven, earth, seas.[7] As his submanager, Adam was to name the various creatures that inhabited this new world:

> Now the LORD God had formed out of the ground all the beasts of the field and all the birds of the air. He brought them to the man to see what he would name them; and whatever the man called each living creature, that was its name. So the man gave names to all the livestock, the birds of the air and all the beasts of the field. (Gen. 2:19–20)

The process of identifying, classifying, and naming made something very apparent to Adam. None of these creatures corresponded to him. Each had its own quality and nature, but none would be capable of partnering with him in his God-given vocation to work and tend creation. Each creature would no doubt provide its own kind of joy and fascination, but none could be a colleague to match and work alongside him.

To meet this need, God created Eve. On seeing her, Adam exclaimed in great excitement:

> This is now bone of my bones
>> and flesh of my flesh;
> she shall be called "woman,"
>> for she was taken out of man. (Gen. 2:23)

She was unlike all the other things God had so far made in Adam's presence. The creatures had been made "out of the ground";[8] she had been made from the body of Adam himself.[9] She was of the same stuff as Adam—a different kind of the same thing. She corresponded to him—he recognized their common substance and nature. She also differed from him—she was "woman" to his "man." From such a combination of likeness and difference comes something profound. The narrator breaks off from these events to relate them to a much wider observation. As the camera pans away from Adam and Eve's newfound joy in each other, we are told what this all means: "For this reason a man will leave his father and mother and be united to his wife, and they will become one flesh" (Gen. 2:24).

Adam and Eve are the first man and wife. In them we see the template of all future marriage. As they are brought together by their Creator, we see much more than a close partnership. They become something greater than just Adam plus Eve. Two persons, yes. Their distinction is not wiped out or blurred together in this union. But these two persons become one flesh.

The oneness of God is the heavenly analogue of the oneness of man and wife.

This is a profound observation because of the way in which it echoes the nature of God himself. The oneness of God is the heavenly analogue of the oneness of man and wife. We find the same particular Hebrew word for "one" in both

Genesis 2 and Deuteronomy 6. By virtue of their marital union, man and woman are able to arrive at a kind of oneness that can reflect the oneness of God the Trinity.

Jesus on marriage

We see this truth echoed by Jesus himself during his earthly ministry. In the course of a discussion about the place of divorce among God's people, he upholds the pattern set out in Genesis 2:

> "Haven't you read," [Jesus] replied, "that at the beginning the Creator 'made them male and female,' and said, 'For this reason a man will leave his father and mother and be united to his wife, and the two will become one flesh'? So they are no longer two, but one. Therefore what God has joined together, let man not separate." (Matt. 19:4–6)

These verses are foundational to our understanding of marriage. There are some important things to discover.

Jesus quotes Genesis 2:24. And when Jesus quotes from the Old Testament, it's not in a here's-some-food-for-thought kind of way. It is not just an interesting perspective to add to the mix. Jesus draws on the Old Testament in the way that two sportsmen might turn to the referee to settle a disputed play. It is the final authority. "Haven't you read?" he says. Whatever Scripture will say on the matter settles it. Case closed.

But Jesus also does two other things with this verse.

Marriage and gender

First, he prefaces it with the fact that, from the very start, God has created humans as men and women. "Haven't you read," Jesus replied, "that at the beginning the Creator 'made them male and female' . . . ?" (Matt. 19:4).

That is the starting point for Jesus' teaching on the issue of marriage. We were created as men and women and have always been created as such, right back "at the beginning." It is part of the original design. This is Jesus' first contention, and it flows right into the second. We are created as gendered beings, and *this is the reason why* we have such a thing as marriage. For *this* reason the man leaves his parents and is united to his wife. Marriage is predicated on our being male and female. Jesus' logic is clear: humanity has been made into two genders, *therefore* there is the phenomenon of marriage. Marriage would not exist were there no difference in gender.[10]

The second thing Jesus does is up the ante by reminding us of precisely whose authority stands behind these verses from Genesis. He quotes the words of the author of Genesis: "For this reason a man will leave his father and mother and be united to his wife, and the two will become one flesh" (Matt. 19:5). But as he does so, he highlights the divine authorship behind them: *He who created said*, "Therefore a man will . . ." The text of Genesis is the word of the Creator.

The next thing we see is Jesus' emphasis on the resulting one flesh: "They are no longer two, but one." Jesus is not saying that man and wife will lose their individual personalities, forever subsumed into one entirely new entity. They have not been merged together. They are not indistinguishable, but they are now designed to be inseparable. A joining process has taken place—expressed and brought about through their sexual union—which cannot be undone.

Moreover, the agency of this joining process is God himself. This one flesh is "what God has joined together." It is not the result of a biological or emotional quirk. Jesus says this union should not be separated by man. The implication is that it could be but shouldn't be. The man and woman who become one flesh are designed and intended by God to remain that way. It is a bond that should be broken only by death. Divorce, in other words, can never be a good thing.

Marriage and family life

It is this one-flesh union that is the context for healthy family life. Consider the following from Malachi: "Has not the LORD made them one? In flesh and spirit they are his. And why one? Because he was seeking godly offspring" (Mal. 2:15).

It is out of this two becoming one that God can provide children. This union is so deep and profound that new life can flow from it. There may again be a parallel with the workings of the Trinity. As Wayne Grudem says, "Although it is not explicitly mentioned in Scripture, the gift of children within marriage, coming from both the father and mother, and subject to the authority of both father and mother, is analogous to the relationship of the Holy Spirit to the Father and Son in the Trinity."[11]

Lots of important insights flow from this.

Marriage and sex

The sexual union that results in one flesh is designed to be enjoyed within the framework of marriage. The becoming one flesh is wrought by God and designed not to be broken. And it makes no sense at all to become one flesh with someone with whom there has been no commitment to stay together. Sex is designed to be enjoyed within the covenant of marriage.

In the movie *Vanilla Sky*, Tom Cruise's character has a one-night stand with Cameron Diaz's character. It sends her into a tailspin, and when eventually she catches up with him she says, "Don't you know that when you sleep with someone, your body makes a promise, whether you do or not?"[12]

Sex is for marriage. Jesus makes this clear in other places

where he lists among other sins that of "sexual immorality."[13] It is a catch-all term for any sexual activity outside of marriage: premarital sex, extramarital sex, and all same-sex sexual activity. While none of these is named specifically, they are all covered by the general term Jesus uses. To suggest that Jesus did not teach on these matters, as some claim today, is simply untrue. Jesus upholds the biblical ethic that the only moral context for sexual activity is marriage.

Marriage and sexuality

And marriage itself is heterosexual. We have already seen that Jesus bases his teaching on marriage on the foundation that there is a difference in gender. You cannot have a marriage between two people of the same sex. A man plus a man may be a deep emotional friendship, but it cannot be a marriage. "Same-sex marriage" is an oxymoron.

These truths can help us in current discussions about sexuality. Over the past couple of years I have heard an increasing number of Christians question why it is that the Bible opposes gay relationships. After all, there are many committed and faithful same-sex partnerships out there. Who are we to say that the quality of those relationships is necessarily inferior to that of a heterosexual couple? We can all think of dysfunctional marriages; why should those be thought of as any better than a happy gay relationship?

This is an understandable and important question. There are a couple of things we need to think about in response. First, the biblical stance on this matter is consistent and clear. Sexual activity between persons of the same gender goes against the purposes for which we were made as sexual beings. Jesus taught that sex is designed to be enjoyed only within (heterosexual) marriage. Sex—including gay sex—outside this context is sinful.

But, second, it is also helpful to see how our understanding of the Trinity provides an added rationale for why this is so. The issue is not really to do with the quality of the relationship but with the depth of the union that can result from it.

Unity in difference, not sameness

The way in which God is one is reflected in the way in which the man and woman are one, and this is hugely significant. God's oneness is not unity in sameness but unity in (complementary) difference. The persons of the Trinity are alike in substance but have eternally been distinct and different. God intends that this kind of unity be echoed in human marriage.

Like the persons of the Trinity, man and woman are made of the same substance and yet are very different from each another. They are different kinds of the same thing. And it is only this combination of likeness and difference that can produce this kind of profound unity. Oneness is found not in sameness but in complementary difference. Two men or two women cannot become one flesh. Only heterosexual intercourse is designed to produce such a union. Homosexual sex may be a means of gratification for each party, but it is not a *union*—two are not becoming one.

I am very conscious of the extent to which this teaching can be painful for many. I am treading on some very delicate ground. For many Christians, this is not an abstract topic. For those who experience attraction to those of the same sex, this is an incredibly sensitive matter. It is hugely personal. I know that living with this issue can bring its own particular pains and difficulties. It is not always easy. But the clarity and wisdom of Scripture can be an enormous encouragement and inspiration. God's word on this matter, no less than any other, is liberating, trustworthy, and *good*.[14]

All of us, without exception, live with a fallen sexuality. All of us are tempted by things for which we were not designed, whether homosexual or heterosexual. We need to keep coming back to our Creator's design for us. The kind of union that finds its fullest human expression in marriage is itself a reflection of what we see in God's own eternal nature: unity in complementary difference.

How to find yourself

The Trinity is not just key for understanding God; it is vital for understanding ourselves. As we reflect on what it means to be made in the image of a trinitarian God, we begin to see who we really are. Loading up the car for a road trip or a backpack for a year abroad are all well and good, but self-discovery starts here: God is Father, Son, and Holy Spirit. All that we were made to be comes from knowing that. Our need for relationships, the importance of serving others, what it means to be sexual beings—all come into true light when seen in relation to our trinitarian God.

6

YOU MAY NOW SERVE THE BRIDE

The Trinity and Gender

ERIC SCHLOSSER'S BOOK *Fast Food Nation* was an exposé of what he called "the dark side" of the fast-food industry. It became a global phenomenon, eventually being made into a movie. The fast-food giants have been on the defensive ever since. The chapter on slaughterhouses put me off burgers for a very long time.

But as well as identifying some of the dubious practices of some well-known fast-food brands, Schlosser's research also introduced him to some of the amazing technological innovation that lies behind this industry. Just take the technology used to produce French fries:

> Conveyor belts took the wet, clean potatoes into a machine that blasted them with steam for twelve seconds, boiled the water under their skins, and exploded their skins off. Then the potatoes were pumped into a preheat tank and shot through a Lamb Water Gun Knife. They emerged as shoestring fries. Four video cameras scrutinized them from

different angles, looking for flaws. When a french fry with a blemish was detected, an optical sorting machine time-sequenced a single burst of compressed air that knocked the bad fry off the production line and onto a separate conveyor belt, which carried it to a machine with tiny automated knives that precisely removed the blemish. And the fry was returned to the main production line.

Sprays of hot water blanched the fries, gusts of hot air dried them, and 25,000 pounds of boiling oil fried them to a slight crisp. Air cooled by compressed ammonia quickly froze them, a computerized sorter that spun like an out-of-control lazy Susan used centrifugal force to align the french fries so that they all pointed in the same direction. The fries were sealed in brown bags, then the bags were loaded by robots into cardboard boxes, and the boxes were stacked by robots onto wooden pallets.[1]

You may be thinking, "That's all well and good, but, as we all know, the chemical composition of soil varies from season to season, so how do they counteract the effects of that?" Good question. And they thought of that. They add sugar to the soil in the autumn and leach it out again in the spring.

The technology is huge and represents the investment of vast sums of money. But the end product shows the payoff: millions and millions of French fries that look, and more importantly taste, exactly the same.

We like uniformity.

Think about it. You could be anywhere on the globe, facing an unfamiliar climate and trying to deal with unfamiliar languages and customs. Immersed in an utterly alien world. And yet step into, say, Starbucks and you know exactly what they'll have and exactly how it will taste. It's the same with countless global chains: fast food, coffee shop, restaurant, hotel—you name it. It doesn't matter if you are in Delhi,

Detroit, Dublin, or Dubai. You are never far away from your favorite frappuccino.

There's something reassuring in all this. Surrounded by unpredictability and unfamiliarity, we find value in this kind of sameness. And we go to considerable lengths to attain it.

As we think further about what it means for God to be triune, we have to come to terms, sooner or later, with a fundamental principle. As we've already seen, the one God is three persons and always has been. These three persons are different; the Father, Son, and Spirit are not the same as one another. They cannot be interchanged. Yet these three persons are one. And so the unity that God has always exhibited and enjoyed, the unity that stands at the center of reality and has for all eternity, this perfect and foundational unity—this unity is of a particular kind.

What we see in God is this: unity not in sameness, but in difference.

It was 5 am and it had woken me up again. I had been in Kuala Lumpur for only a few days, but so far each of them had started involuntarily at this hour. We were staying in a guest house, and just around the corner the local mosque was broadcasting its dawn call to prayer.

I'll be honest—I'm not at my best at 5 am. My initial thoughts were not of peace and goodwill toward my fellow man. But once the grumpiness had eventually subsided and I had become reconciled to the fact that the day had now irrevocably started, the call to prayer got me thinking.

I'm not much of an expert on Islam, but it struck me that the call to prayer I'd heard might be a pretty good musical expression of what Muslims believe about God. Allah is understood to be a solitary entity, a singularity. In the language of people who know these things, he is a monad. (Note to self: a *monad* is an irreducible, singular entity or being. A *nomad* is someone looking for affordable accommodation anywhere in London.)

This, it seemed to me, was what the call to prayer was reflecting musically – aural theology, if you like. It was the cry of a lone voice (in this case, I think, prerecorded). No instrumentation, no accompaniment of any kind, no polyphony. Just a singular melody.

It is surely no accident that societies that have been significantly influenced by biblical Christianity, and by extension the Christian understanding of the Trinity, have produced complex polyphony. One thinks, for example, of the music of a devout Christian like J. S. Bach. It would be natural for there to be a relationship between a society's theology and its music. Interestingly, in his book on the Trinity, Robert Letham notes that touring orchestras tend to be in less demand in strongly Islamic cultures.[2]

If this is so, then it should not surprise us. The God of Scripture has revealed himself as triune: unity in three different persons. Theological harmony, a beautiful musical integration.

Unity in diversity. This is going to be significant. We'll get God wrong if we don't grasp this. We'll also get some other key things wrong. As we have come to expect, what God shows us about himself is going to have all sorts of important practical implications for us. We are not just to notice this aspect of what it means for God to be triune, but to live in the light of it.

We are not left in the dark as to how this applies. This feature of God's unity is applied directly in the New Testament to two areas of human life: gender and church—two topics of huge importance. We'll consider how the Trinity helps us as we think about gender and, if you're still around, we'll consider church in the next chapter.

Here's Paul: "Now I want you to realise that the head of every man is Christ, and the head of the woman is man, and the head of Christ is God?" (1 Cor. 11:3).

Paul lists three things that are the head of other things:

1. Christ is the head of man.
2. Man is the head of woman.
3. God is the head of Christ.

Okay, so Paul has just mentioned the words "man," "head," and "woman" in the same sentence.[3] Wherever he's about to go with this, we immediately feel ourselves stepping onto suspect ground as far as Western culture is concerned. It feels a little like Paul might be about to roll back all that has been achieved in women's rights over the last century, and some of you are about to put the book down. But believe me, he isn't, so please don't. Or, at the very least, please stick around long enough to see just one thing. What you do after that is up to you.

Whatever Paul means by "headship"—and if that term is making your eyes bleed, then please set it aside for a moment and let's call it "man-to-woman-ship" for now until we've worked out what we are dealing with—it flows out of how God exists as Trinity.

Whatever man is supposed to be to woman is meant to correspond to how God (the Father) is to Christ (the Son). The dynamic of this relationship within the Trinity is something we are to map onto our relationship as men and women. In other words, to properly understand what it means to have been created as men and women, we need to understand how the Father and Son relate to each other. Our view of gender needs to flow from our view of the Trinity.

This being so, what is actually at stake in this discussion is not whether we find ourselves in step or out of step with surrounding culture, but whether we find ourselves in or out of step with how God works as God. So be honest: which of those two things matters more to you? Who would you rather end up clashing with: the culture that surrounds you, or the God who made you? We will trace out the shape of the Father and Son's relationship within the Trinity. It is beautiful: both Father and Son exult in it. It is to be the analogue of our human relationships as men and women. So let's be clear: if we reject *that*—where this all ends up going in our understanding of gender—we will be rejecting the very way that God chooses to be God. Like I said, what you choose to do with this teaching is up to you, but at least know what the stakes are before making up your mind.

THE RELATIONSHIP BETWEEN FATHER AND SON

There exists, somewhere deep in my psyche, an unshakeable conviction that I am a "maps person." A GPS or list of directions is not for me. All I need is a casual glance at a map before heading off. I have, according to this conviction, a virtually flawless internal compass. (I can confidently assert that I am oriented in a south-southwest direction as I type this.) I also possess, where cartographic information is concerned, unusual powers of retention. At least that's the theory.

The reality presents a rather different case. It is a curiosity of my self-belief where directions are concerned that it has endured, unwavering, in the face of so much evidence to the contrary. Many times I have found myself in places that were patently not my destination. On one memorable occasion my navigational instincts resulted in my having to execute a U-turn on a railway station platform.

There are times when we need to come back and look at something again, this time more closely. The first glance might have given a helpful overall sense of where things lie. But closer study is needed if we are to find our way around at street level. It is true for me (I need to learn) when it comes to maps and directions. And it is also true when it comes to the Trinity.

We have already seen something of the equality and distinction that exist between the persons of the Trinity. But a closer look is needed—a closer look at the equality and difference between the Son and the Father.

Probing more deeply into their equality

When it comes to the equality between the members of the Trinity, Bruce Ware hits the nail smack on the head:

> There is one and only one God, eternally existing and fully expressed in three Persons, the Father, the Son, and the Holy Spirit. Each member of the Godhead is equally God, each is eternally God, and each is fully God—not three gods but three Persons of the one Godhead. Each Person is equal in essence as each possesses fully the identically same, eternal divine nature, yet each is also an eternal and distinct personal expression of the one undivided nature.[4]

Father and Son are each fully divine. The Son is as much God as the Father is. They share the same nature and same substance; they are made of the same "stuff." The words of the Nicene Creed help to shed to a little more light on this. Jesus, we are reminded, is

> the only Son of God,
> eternally begotten of the Father,

God from God, Light from Light,
true God from true God,
begotten, not made,
of one Being with the Father.[5]

"Begotten, not made" is an important distinction. C. S. Lewis explains why.

> When you beget, you beget something of the same kind as yourself. A man begets human babies, a beaver begets little beavers and a bird begets eggs which turn into little birds. But when you make, you make something of a different kind from yourself. A bird makes a nest, a beaver builds a dam, a man makes a wireless set. . . . What God begets is God; just as what man begets is man. What God creates is not God; just as what man creates is not man.[6]

Jesus is fully divine. The Father and Son are equal in essence and divinity.

Probing more deeply into their difference

The Father is not the Son and the Son is not the Father. There are differences in their roles. They play different parts within the divine economy. And this means that there is a particular shape to their relationship.

Difference during Jesus' earthly ministry

We see this in operation during the time when Jesus was on the earth. Consider the following: "I do nothing on my own but speak just what the Father has taught me. The one who sent me is with me; he has not left me alone, for I always do what pleases him" (John 8:28–29).

The Father teaches the Son what the Son is to say. The

Father is the one who sends the Son. We see the Father being the one who leads and the Son the one who follows that lead. And the Son does what will please the Father. *Always* does what pleases the Father; Jesus is not selective in this. He doesn't exercise his own discretion at this point. He is not even pleasing generally. But always. In everything. No exceptions. In all he did, Jesus showed unswerving commitment to bringing pleasure to his Father. So Bruce Ware says, "The eternal Son of the Father is both '*God* the Son' and 'God the Son.'"[7] Equal in divinity, submissive in role.

We see this again later in John's gospel: "I love the Father and I do exactly what my Father has commanded me" (John 14:31).

This is the shape of their relationship. The Father sends, teaches, commands. The Son responds and obeys. And this dynamic is never reversed. We never see the Son commanding the Father or sending the Father. We never see the Father obeying the Son or following him.

We also need to see that this is not a cold, heartless dynamic. The Father is not some faceless autocrat firing off instructions to a distant underling. Jesus is not some lackey trapped in a thankless existence that he would love to break out of. Listen again to what Jesus says: "I love the Father and I do exactly what my Father has commanded me." Jesus is not under the thumb or serving his Father through clenched teeth. There is a delight for him in obeying the Father, precisely because by doing so he is able to express his love for the Father. As he walked this earth, it was his pleasure to do so in full obedience to all that the Father had commanded him.

But this arrangement was not temporary.

Difference in eternity past

When I organize interviews for those applying to become ministry apprentices at our church, I and the other interviewers normally work out in advance who is going to cover which questions. I like to take the chatty, tell-us-about-your-hobbies questions that we tend to ask during the first part of the interview. And I like my female colleague to take the deeper theological questions; she tends to sound more gentle and less threatening. It's our version of good cop/bad cop.

It is not like that with the Trinity. As we have seen, before the birth of Jesus there was not a conversation within the Trinity about who was going to come to earth and who was going to stay behind, who was going to take the "Son" role and who the "Father" role. No, the Father-Son dynamic we see during Jesus' earthly ministry has actually existed for all eternity. We have already considered these well-known words: "For God so loved the world that he gave his one and only Son, that whoever believes in him shall not perish but have eternal life" (John 3:16).

Before the birth of Jesus there was a sender and a Son, one who initiated in love and one who followed in obedience. It is part of the Father's father-ness to send and part of the Son's son-ness to respond. The Father and Son have always had these roles.

Or again, "What about the one whom the Father set apart as his very own and sent into the world?" (John 10:36). The dynamic we saw during the earthly life of Jesus was not an anomaly, but a reflection of the dynamic that has existed between the Father and Son for all eternity.

And will continue to exist.

Difference in eternity future

The exaltation and ascension of Jesus after his death and resurrection is not a graduation from being the Son of the Father to some supposedly better, less submissive role. In fact, his very exaltation is itself "to the glory of God the Father" (Phil. 2:11).

Elsewhere Paul looks forward to the day when everything in creation will be subject to the Son.

> Then the end will come, when [Christ] hands over the kingdom to God the Father after he has destroyed all dominion, authority and power. . . . When he has done this, then the Son himself will be made subject to him who put everything under him, so that God may be all in all. (1 Cor. 15:24, 28)

Creation will be entirely subject to the Son. Everything will have been put under his feet. But it is the Father who has put everything under him, and the Son will hand over the kingdom to the Father and will himself be subjected to the Father. The dynamic we have seen all along will continue into the future forever.

So the relationship between Father and Son has a particular shape. They share the same essence and divine nature and yet express that divine nature differently. They are Father and Son; there is authority and submission. This shape has always existed and will always continue to exist. And, returning to where we began, Paul sums up this shape using the concept of headship: the head of Christ is God the Father.

Headship in the Trinity

Having seen this dynamic at work between the Father and the Son, we can now begin to anticipate what Paul means by "head."

"Head" in Paul's day could refer to the same things it does today:

- The peculiar cranial protrusion on top of your shoulders.
- The origin or source of something. (I grew up just down the road from a place called Riverhead, though I have yet to find any evidence of a river starting there.)

- A position of leadership and responsibility—someone might be the head of a company or of a department or a school, or even the head of a state.

Although Bible-believing Christians sometimes differ on this, it seems clear from what we have already seen that there is an authority-submission dynamic in relation to the Father and Son. And so it makes the most sense for this to be the kind of headship Paul is talking about here. It fits in with what he says elsewhere about men and women, where the context is clearly one of differing roles and authority. "Wives, submit to your husbands as to the Lord. For the husband is the head of the wife as Christ is the head of the church" (Eph. 5:22–23).

Headship here is clearly not referring to the husband being the "source" of his wife, but of his having a position of authority over her. It is a headship to which the wife is to submit. This sense of headship also fits in with the first part of 1 Corinthians 11, where, again, the issue concerns the woman being under the authority of the man (see verse 10).

In fact, this has been Paul's point in 1 Corinthians 11:3. Just as the Father exercises headship over the Son, so too the husband is to have headship over his wife. The dynamic of the husband/wife relationship is to take its cue from, and correspond to, the dynamic of God the Father and God the Son, where this dynamic has eternally existed.

Implications of this relationship

Before we get into how this dynamic is reflected between men and women, we need to step back and draw a few conclusions from what we have seen about headship from its existence in the Trinity.

Equality and difference are not mutually exclusive

Equality and difference exist together within the Trinity and have always done so. There is no tension between them. They in no way threaten God's unity, as if this depended on some kind of precarious standoff between the two. The opposite is in fact the case. The complementarity of the persons of the Trinity is what constitutes God's unity. His unity is not in uniformity or sameness, but in difference. The result is beautiful, relational harmony.

Within the Trinity, headship and submission do not involve inequality

There is always the potential for human expressions of this dynamic to lead to the demeaning of one party, but in such cases the wrong sort of headship is being promoted—one that does not faithfully reflect the loving headship of God the Father. The Son is never demeaned by the Father's headship. He is not inferior because he submits to the Father, any more than Father is superior because he has authority over the Son. In fact, both headship and submission are means of delight to Father and Son, and expressions of their love for each other.

Headship and submission are not intrinsically bad

God is good. Nothing in his nature is flawed. What he exhibits is perfection. And that includes all the dynamics we see within the Trinity. We have already noted that the headship and submission of Father and Son were not temporary roles adopted only for Jesus' earthly ministry as a sort of regrettable necessity. They always existed, and always will, as eternal qualities within the Godhead. It is always possible for humans to twist and distort the good things of reality into a means of evil. But this does not diminish the goodness of those things in the first place.

Often in Western culture two people are considered to be equal only if they are allowed to do exactly the same things. But this is not so within the Trinity. Equality is not sameness. And the different roles being exercised are how we end up with the God we know and love.

THE RELATIONSHIP BETWEEN THE MAN AND WOMAN

Back to 1 Corinthians 11. Paul wants us to see that there is correspondence between the relationship of the Father and the Son and the intended relationship between man and woman. Just as we saw equality and headship/submission within the Trinity, so too we see it between the sexes.

Equality and difference

The Bible shows us the equal worth and value of the persons of the Trinity; it also shows us the same of men and women. Just as with the Father and Son, so also men and women are made of the same stuff. Eve, cried Adam in joy, is "bone of my bones and flesh of my flesh" (Gen. 2:23). She shared his human nature and corresponded to him physically.

We have already seen from the creation account that men and women are created equal. Both are made in the image of God and share this dignity equally. Neither gender is more or less the image of God than the other. There is no inferiority of one sex and superiority of the other. Wayne Grudem can therefore say,

> Wherever men are thought to be better than women, wherever
> husbands act as selfish dictators, wherever wives are forbidden
> to have their own jobs outside the home or to vote or to own

property or to be educated, wherever women are treated as inferior, wherever there is abuse or violence against women or rape or female infanticide or polygamy or harems, the biblical truth of equality in the image of God is being denied.[8]

Tragically, there is no shortage of examples of these scenarios today. It is a reminder of how urgently this message needs to be heard in our world. There are many places where baby girls are considered of less value than baby boys, leading to cases of the former being aborted, killed, or abandoned. India and China, for example, have wildly disproportionate gender ratios, with tens of millions of women effectively missing from the population.[9]

We are equal. No one should feel particularly proud or ashamed that he is a man or that she is a woman, as if one were better or worse. Both equally have the dignity of bearing the image of God.

But equality, as we have seen, does not mean sameness. Adam and Eve are not interchangeable. They are made of the same stuff, but in a way that means there is complementarity. Kathy Keller is worth quoting at length:

> Using all the qualifiers in the world, in general, as a whole and across the spectrum, men have a gift of independence, a "sending" gift. They look outward. They initiate. Under sin, these traits can become either an alpha male individualism, if this capacity is turned into an idol, or dependence, if the calling is utterly rejected and the opposite embraced in rebellion. The first sin is hypermasculinity, while the second sin is a rejection of masculinity.
>
> Using all the qualifiers in the world, on the whole and across the spectrum, women have a gift of interdependence, a "receiving" gift. They are inwardly perceptive. They nurture.

Under sin, these traits can become either a clinging dependence, if attachment is turned into an idol, or individualism, if the calling is utterly rejected and the opposite embraced in rebellion. The first sin is hyperfemininity, while the second sin is a rejection of femininity.[10]

Headship in male-female relationships

As we have seen, there is headship. The head of Christ is God the Father, and the head of the woman is man.

We see this applied to two contexts. In Ephesians 5 we see the headship of men within marriage: "Wives, submit to your husbands as to the Lord. For the husband is the head of the wife as Christ is the head of the church" (Eph. 5:22–23).

In 1 Corinthians 11 we see male headship within the local church. Let me quote the passage in full.

> Now I want you to realise that the head of every man is Christ, and the head of the woman is man, and the head of Christ is God. Every man who prays or prophesies with his head covered dishonours his head. And every woman who prays or prophesies with her head uncovered dishonours her head—it is just as though her head were shaved. If a woman does not cover her head, she should have her hair cut off; and if it is a disgrace for a woman to have her hair cut or shaved off, she should cover her head. A man ought not to cover his head, since he is the image and glory of God; but the woman is the glory of man. For man did not come from woman, but woman from man; neither was man created for woman, but woman for man. For this reason, and because of the angels, the woman ought to have a sign of authority on her head. (1 Cor. 11:3–10)

This passage is part of a wider section dealing with various areas of local church life, such as the administration of the

Lord's Supper and the exercise of spiritual gifts. But here Paul's concern seems to be the importance of headship of men in the church being acknowledged in the way men and women present and comport themselves.[11]

I am conscious that in both these areas—church life and marriage—the issue of male headship has felled entire forests. There is legitimate room for discussion about what it might look like in practice. Our main concern here is that we see how it comes from the trinitarian nature of God. But before we go, let's consider some important implications.

All of us are under headship

It is not as if one gender is under a head and the other is not. Paul is not saying that women need headship and that men don't, as if men are somehow above that sort of thing. Both men and women have a head. The head in each case is different, but each sex alike is under authority. So no one is being demeaned. God the Son has a head. For woman to be under the head of man is no more demeaning than for God the Son to be under the head of the Father, or for man to be under the head of Christ. All of us are under authority.

Christ is the example for us all

The Son is under the headship of the Father. He is also the head over every man. He is therefore an example both of headship and of submission to headship. He is an example for both sexes to follow: an example to men of how to exercise loving headship, and an example to women of loving submission to headship. All of us alike are to look to him as our model.

Male headship is to correspond to the loving headship of God the Father

Headship is to be marked by responsibility. There is a general sense in which guys are to take the initiative. This is particularly true in marriage, but is also true more generally in a lower-key kind of way. Men are to be especially looking out for the spiritual welfare of others and taking a lead in corporate spiritual life, not least in prayer.

Headship is also to be marked by kindness. The Father loves exalting the Son. He delights in him. There is authority, but it is not authoritarian. It is other-person-centered.

So, women, if you think it is demeaning to be under the headship of man, you have not understood the Trinity, in which this pattern of headship and submission is not only present but is a beautiful reality. The headship Paul speaks of for you is akin to that of the Father's over the Son.

And men, if at this point you are smiling to yourself with a goofy grin on your face because this sounds like a fun deal, you have also not understood the Trinity. It does not mean you get to be a jerk to women. The headship required of you is to be one of service, care, and love.

It is only by understanding the triune nature of God that men and women can truly learn to relate rightly to one another. It is only the Trinity that can give us a true framework of difference and equality going together, of the unity that comes from diversity being prized and cherished and therefore from people being encouraged to fulfill their vocation as men and women.

We see this most perhaps clearly by considering what would happen if we lost a trinitarian understanding of God. God would not be triune; he would just be a divine singularity, utter undifferentiated oneness. That would become our understanding of what is ultimate. And the presence of two different genders would be something of an obstacle to that. And so, inevitably, the physically stronger of the two sexes would assert itself over the other, forcing it indoors and away from visibility in the public sphere. Without the Trinity, one of the sexes will end up putting a veil over the other.

Similarly, if we retain a sense of the goodness of diversity and difference but lose sight of the concept of that diversity being put into the service of unity, we will also end up with a dysfunctional understanding of gender. We will affirm every expression of diversity, but without a rationale for how it could ever produce an integrated whole.

But the Bible sounds neither the air-horn blast of uniformity nor the white noise of utter diversity.

There will be diversity aplenty, but with no sense of order, still less of any concept of headship. The result will be a denial of the idea of gender as being fixed and definite. It will become an entirely fluid concept, something as changeable (in theory, at least) as hair coloring.

But the Bible sounds neither the air-horn blast of uniformity nor the white noise of utter diversity. There are neither McPeople nor sub-people. Instead we hear music. The harmony of unity in diversity. The divine orchestra of the Trinity itself and the echo played back by men and women made in its image.

SHOWING GOD
TO THE WORLD

The Trinity and Church

OUR CHURCH OFFICE was once sent a free calendar by
a denominational insurance company. Each month featured the
picture of a different church and some reasons why you should
visit it. In pretty much every case it had to do with the heritage
and setting of the building. January's church had a wonderful
Norman tower going for it. April's still had the pews from the
twelfth century (a pretty good reason *not* to visit it, if you ask
me). My favorite was the church that could still boast that its
rafters were home to a colony of bats. (I'll make no jokes about
our Thursday afternoon retirees' meeting.)

While I would hardly expect good theology from an
insurance company freebie, it still got me thinking about how
much of the thinking out there seems to miss the point of
what churches have to offer. In my part of the world, it seems
to come down more or less to pretty architecture.

We could, of course, probably offer some more compelling things a church might have going for it: great music, say, or

thought-provoking teaching, or a sense of support. But there's a better one that comes up several times in the New Testament, and it's probably nowhere near the radar for most Christians.

The church is a visual aid of the Trinity. Something of God's three-in-oneness is reflected in the life of his people.

Along with marriage, the church is God's illustration to us of his trinitarian life.

The apostle Paul gives us a number of images to help us understand the local church. It is a household: our fellow believers are not just members of the same Christian club, but are our brothers and sisters in Christ. Or it's like a building: an entity that is meant to be built up and strengthened in its service to Christ. Or it's like a bride: not just an institution with mission statements and a constitution, but a body pledged to Christ and called to be faithful to him. But the image Paul spends most time on is the human body.

> *Along with marriage, the church is God's illustration to us of his trinitarian life.*

THE CHURCH'S UNITY

The church is like a body in its unity. Each church is a single entity: lots of people, perhaps, and a variety of ministries, committees, teams, and groups. But all comprising one church body, just like a human body—made up of all sorts of bits and pieces but all working together as one.

> The body is a unit, though it is made up of many parts; and though all its parts are many, they form one body. So it is with Christ. For we were all baptised by one Spirit into one body—

whether Jews or Greeks, slave or free— and we were all given the one Spirit to drink. (1 Cor. 12:12–13)

Unity in the context of diversity

The human body has a bewildering variety of parts: bones, cells, muscles, organs, and so on. But however many parts go into it, it is demonstrably one entity. When you see someone walking your way, you don't say to yourself, "Here come 200 bones, 650 skeletal muscles, and 50 trillion cells." You say, "Here comes Jeff." For all its many components, the human body is organized biologically into a clear unity.

It is the same with the church. It is one unit, a single entity.

Its members may be extraordinarily diverse. Paul references Jews and Greeks, slave and free—ethnicity and economic status being just two axes along which we can often find huge variety. Yet there is an overriding unity.

Unity from God

And Paul is clear where this unity has come from. It has been created by God; it is not of human devising. It may be expressed by a doctrinal statement of belief, a church constitution, a denominational confession, or articles of faith. But it is not created by those things. It comes from God—specifically from his Spirit.

Paul says that the Holy Spirit has baptized fellow Christians into the same body. We have all been "given the one Spirit to drink." The same Spirit of God has been given to all of us. And he has given us to one another. Not like when parents and their friends throw their kids into the same room, tell them to play nicely, and then step back and hope they will get along. No, the Spirit has actually bound us together. We have all been baptized into this Spirit, united to him in a way that unites us to one another so profoundly that we are now parts of the same body.

And sharing one body, we are to share the same mindset. Here's Paul again: "Your attitude should be the same as that of Christ Jesus" (Phil. 2:5).

Literally, Paul is saying, "Let the mind be in you that was in Christ Jesus." Have the same mindset, the same attitude. As Christians in the same church we are to have the same approach: "being like-minded, having the same love, being one in spirit and purpose" (Phil. 2:2). However different we may be in our gifting, temperament, and natural passions, we are to be pulling in the same direction.

Again, this shared mindset is not something we need to cook up ourselves. It is not established by a church-wide vote or a specially commissioned steering group. The mindset we are to share is that of Christ himself.

It is a mindset that puts others before self. Jesus is the great exemplar of service:

> Who, being in very nature God,
>   did not consider equality with God
>   something to be grasped,
> but made himself nothing,
>   taking the very nature of a servant,
>   being made in human likeness. (Phil. 2:6–7)

That mark of a healthy human relationship—being other-person-centered—is especially to characterize the relationships of the local church. We above all should most reflect this principle, for we above all have been exposed to the radical self-sacrifice of Christ. If he is truly our example and goal, then his attitude of service will become ours too. We will increasingly be learning to look to "the interests of others" (v. 4), to do "nothing out of selfish ambition or vain conceit" (v. 3).

Becoming what we worship

We always become what we worship.[1] It is true of all people, irrespective of what is being worshipped. What we most esteem, we will emulate. What we think of as being foundational, we will build our lives upon. What we consider of utmost value, we will put at the center of everything. It will shape us. We will conform ourselves to it. It will be our bottom line, our non-negotiable. It might be power or popularity or success or the accumulation of things. It might be the ability to control our destiny or the achievements of our children or the acceptance of our friends. It might be a religious deity: Allah of the Koran or Vishnu of the Hindu scriptures.

But if it is Christ of the Bible, then the true mark of genuine faith in him will not be what we say or do, but what we become. If we truly worship him, we will become like him—self-giving and servant-hearted. We worship the one who said, "I am among you as one who serves" (Luke 22:27). Our fundamental outlook will be dominated not by our being served by others, but by our being of service to them. Imagine a church full of such people. What an amazing prospect! No wonder Christians sharing this mindset are what make Paul's "joy complete" (Phil. 2:2). Sharing such an attitude not only makes for better life together (though it undoubtedly does), but it is the sign that we are truly living out the unity that the Spirit has given us.

Christ expressed his unity with the Father not by living for himself and his own interests, but instead by committing himself to the interests of others—chief among them the Father's glory (Phil. 2:11). To the extent that we follow this pattern we reflect something of the dynamic of the Trinity.

Our unity is to take after the Trinity. So too is our diversity.

THE CHURCH'S DIVERSITY

The unity of the church is found and expressed in its diversity. The church is a body, and each Christian is a part of that body. But Paul wants us to notice just how different these individual parts are and how that relates positively to the unity the body enjoys. We can be one precisely because we are different.

This is a key mark of any healthy church and it has its grounding in the Trinity. Our unity is in diversity and not in uniformity, in difference and not in sameness.

As Paul comes to stress the diversity of the parts of the church's body, he does so by referencing its grounds in the trinitarian nature of God. "There are different kinds of gifts, but the same Spirit. There are different kinds of service, but the same Lord. There are different kinds of working, but the same God works all of them in all men" (1 Cor. 12:4–6).

Paul talks about the various kinds of activity the parts will undertake. There are different kinds of gifts, of service, of working. We will not all share the same spiritual vocation. We are not identical cogs in the same machine. And overriding this variety is the one God who enables us all. There is the same Spirit, the same Lord, the same God. *Lord* and *God* are favorite expressions of Paul's for the Father and the Son—Paul is talking here about the Trinity.

Paul is not saying that "gifts" are exclusively the department of the Spirit, "forms of service" the department only of the Son, and "different workings" the preserve of just the Father, as if each were an entirely separate concern and overseen in isolation by a different person of the Trinity. His point, rather, is this: behind the unity in diversity of the church is its heavenly analogue, the unity in diversity of the Trinity, and the operational diversity of the church is a reflection of the Trinity.

Christians, then, are given a variety of ways to be a blessing and service to the body, the church. No Christian is an exception to this: "Now to each one the manifestation of the Spirit is given for the common good" (1 Cor. 12:7).

There is a whole range of ways in which we can be of service to one another. Paul lists some of them in the next few verses:

> To one there is given through the Spirit the message of wisdom, to another the message of knowledge by means of the same Spirit, to another faith by the same Spirit, to another gifts of healing by that one Spirit, to another miraculous powers, to another prophecy, to another distinguishing between spirits, to another speaking in different kinds of tongues, and to still another the interpretation of tongues.
> (1 Cor. 12: 8–10)

In other parts of the New Testament we find other lists that are slightly different from this one. Other gifts not mentioned here are mentioned there, while others mentioned here are excluded there.[2] So what we have here is not the spiritual equivalent of a set menu, but a sample of just some of the gifts. The list is not exhaustive, but representative. Paul's point is not to provide a checklist, but to illustrate diversity. One body, many parts; one church, different gifts. In the verses that follow, Paul spells out two significant implications of this.

One body, many parts; one church, different gifts.

Don't look down on your gifts

The church is a mix. Far from this being accidental, God has intended it to be this way. We are meant to be different from one another. But wherever there is a mix, there will always be some who feel inferior.

For most of us, our foot is not our most attractive feature. It is possible for someone to be complimented on having nice hair or a nice smile. But I've yet to hear of anyone being complimented on having nice *feet*. Toes can be chubby or spindly and generally pointing in different directions. There may be unsightly tufts of hair in all the wrong places. And there are the nails, on some people so cracked and broken it's as if they've been partially detonated. Feet tend to look like a genetic experiment that has gone horribly wrong.

Paul may have thought so too, since it's the toe he imagines having some esteem issues: "If the foot should say, 'Because I am not a hand, I do not belong to the body,' it would not for that reason cease to be part of the body" (1 Cor. 12:15).

The poor old foot could easily feel inferior, especially when compared to the hand. It might feel less useful, less "handy" (sorry). There is loads a hand can do that a foot can't. In writing this chapter it is my hands that have done the key work, not my feet. The hands can pick up books, turn pages, take notes, and type words onto the screen. My feet may as well have been on sabbatical. But the foot is no less a part of the body. It was my feet that got me to the study, that took me to the bookshelf and conveyed me back to my desk. They were not as uninvolved as we might first think. Trying to do the whole enterprise without the use of my feet would have been a very different undertaking.

And that's the lesson. It is easy to look at the more obvious gifts and feel useless for not possessing them, especially in a church context. We find ourselves saying, "I'm not musical. I don't play piano or guitar. I can't even find a note on a kazoo." Or, "I'm not someone who knows what to say when someone else is in distress." Or, "I'm not good in front of a crowd; I could never stand up in front of the church and give a reading or say a prayer." Or, "I'm not good with words; I'm no good at expressing myself. Things never come out the right way and it always leads to a muddle. I could never give a talk or lead a Bible study." And in each case we easily conclude, "I'm not really any use to anyone in this church. I can't be part of the action like others are."

But however you feel when you compare yourself to others, you are as much a part of the body as anyone else. For every visible thing that happens in church, there is a bunch of behind-the-scenes, invisible stuff that needs to have happened first. Just for a regular Sunday meeting at my church, orders of service need to have been put together, printed off, folded, and handed out. Rooms need to have been unlocked, equipment set out and prepared. Music needs to have been chosen, printed, and rehearsed. Someone will have organized whose turn it is to read, pray, welcome, play or sing in the band, serve refreshments, help with the kids' ministry, operate the sound system, and all manner of other things. All that is before I can even stand up and start the meeting. And that's just the stuff off the top of my head.

It is no accident that this is how it works. The church is meant to be diverse. We are meant to be different from one another and to need one another. For God is the one who has made us diverse. "In fact God has arranged the parts in the body, every one of them, just as he wanted them to be. If they were all one part, where would the body be?" (1 Cor. 12:18–19).

We need our differences, our diversity. If my local church were full of people who were just like me, then on a good day maybe one percent of church life would work well. The rest would be a catastrophe. Our unity is found in difference, not in sameness.

If we look around at our brothers and sisters and feel inferior, we need the encouragement of these verses. God does not want you to be someone else. He made you as you because he wants to use your "you-ness." So there's no need for envy. But there's also a challenge here. If you are no less part of the body than the next person, then you have no reason not to be involved and serving others. If there's no place for envy, then there's also no place for detachment. The church is designed to reflect the unity in diversity of the Trinity.

If we lose sight of this perspective, we risk our churches becoming monochrome. Maturity will be understood in terms of trying to make everyone a certain kind of Christian. There will be a cultural and vocational flatness. Christians will look and sound the same. They'll be encouraged into the same kind of ministry. A particular gifting will be the hallmark of the spiritually advanced. In some churches today it is the gift of tongues. In others it is the gift of teaching—those really committed to the gospel will become "Bible teachers." Christians lacking that particular gift will be left feeling that they have far less to offer the body. In both cases Paul's point in this passage is being missed. All gifts are needed and God has made us diverse for a reason!

Don't look down on others' gifts

If in any crowd there are those feeling inferior, there will also be those who feel superior. People who think they matter more, that they are more special. They are like the eye: "The eye cannot say to the hand, 'I don't need you!'" (1 Cor. 12:21).

It is easy for those whose gifting is higher profile to get an unhealthy kick out of that. "Everyone else sees what I do," they might think to themselves, even if subconsciously. "My role is particularly important. Everyone here needs me to be doing this. Lucky them to have me on board!"

The message for the superior is the same: everyone is needed. Everyone. You need others as much as others need you. Don't look down on others just because their ministry might be more discreet or menial in your eyes.

It is right that not everyone has the same kind of visibility in church. Some parts of the body are particularly tender. You might feel as though your life has been a mess: perhaps it's your home life or your relationships that have not been running smoothly. Maybe you have struggled with a significant addiction that has left you feeling somewhat vulnerable. It might be that you carry within you a significant emotional wound. You might feel like one of those parts that Paul says "seem to be weaker" (v. 22). And yet those very parts are "indispensable." What feels like your weakness might be the very thing God uses to make you a blessing to others. I can think of people who have struggled though the pain of losing a child, or marital breakdown, or having been abused, or addiction, or chronic depression and yet have been able to exercise a powerful ministry to others with similar struggles.

Other parts Paul describes as being "unpresentable" (v. 23). Let's face it, there are parts of our body we don't show to other people. I'm typing these words while sitting in a bustling coffee shop. It is well into winter, and the shop is nice and toasty inside. In fact, I'm sitting just near a large fireplace and have been progressively getting too hot. Various outer layers of my clothing have already been shed and lie strewn over the empty chair next to me. But however much I might want to strip off, there is an agreed minimum of clothing that needs to remain in place, irrespective of how hot it is. It's not that those parts of the body are insignificant. But they have no public role to play!

There are some in the church community who are precious to us, but who it would not be appropriate to stick in front of everyone with a microphone in their face. They need to be less visible. I know of dear Christians who have struggled with suicidal feelings and needed hospitalization as a result. For such friends, the first steps back into our Sunday fellowship will be very tentative—slipping in after the service has begun and leaving just before it has finished. They will be ready to see one or two of us to begin with, but not everyone. Brothers and sisters like this will need to be less visible for now, for their own sakes. But they are no less valuable to our church family because of that.

We are different and need to play different roles in the life of the church family. Some will be more visible, others less so. But all of us are needed. There is no one in the fellowship we can look down on, no type of person we can just do without. Think of your own church fellowship. You need these particular others whom God has put around you, even if you (and they) don't know it.

There is an oft quoted African proverb: "It takes a village to raise a child."[3] It reminds us that there is a communal side to our development. We are not isolated or self-sufficient; healthy growth will involve a range of people. This is just as true of our spiritual development. If it takes a village to raise a child, it takes a church to raise a Christian. Like it or not, you need others and others need you. Going to church will not make you a Christian, but it is very hard to see how you can really go on as a Christian without church.

Being a body

The church, in all its diversity, acts as one body. God has combined us into one unit. What affects one of us affects us all. "If one part suffers, every part suffers with it; if one part is honoured, every part rejoices with it" (1 Cor. 12:26).

When one part suffers, all parts suffer. I stubbed my toe the other day while padding about at home barefooted. I was pulling a door closed, and as the door completed its arc it took with it a generous amount of nail from my big toe. Lavish amounts of bleeding followed. But more than my toe was affected–other parts of the body responded too. My eyes watered. I grabbed the toe with my hands and proceeded to hop on the other leg. My mouth produced a noise unusual both in volume and in pitch. It was not enough to say my toe hurt—*I* hurt.

So it is with the church. When one part hurts, we all feel it. When someone comes down with a serious illness, when someone's marriage or family falls apart, when someone is bereaved or loses his job, it hurts us all because we are all part of the same spiritual body. What weakens or distresses one weakens and distresses us all.

Similarly, when one part rejoices we all feel it. When someone leads a friend to Christ or experiences a breakthrough with a besetting sin or finally gets a much prayed-for job or achieves some kind of success, we all celebrate. It brings joy to the whole body. We respond as one.

There's a great illustration of this in the hit TV series *The West Wing*. A junior staffer in the White House has leaked a sensitive quote to the press. Communications Director Toby Ziegler, a character not normally known for his happy demeanor even at the best of times, assembles all the junior staff and is about to let rip. But instead he finds himself speaking about the unity they share as fellow White House staffers:

> We're a group. We're a team. From the President and Leo on through, we're a team. We win together and we lose together; we celebrate and we mourn together. And defeats are softened and victories sweeter because we did them together. You're

my guys and I'm yours. And there's really nothing I wouldn't do for you.[4]

He could be talking about a church. For all our variety, the Spirit has bound us together as one body. We have a stake in one another.

Christ's body

But Paul doesn't leave the discussion there. He has a final punch in store. The church is not just *like* a body; it *is* a body. It is, in fact, the very body of Christ (1 Cor. 12:27).

Christ's physical body is in heaven where he ascended. But the church is his spiritual body here on earth. This is huge. It means that what we do to one another in church, we do to the body of Christ.

Paul knew something of this firsthand. When, in his earlier life as a Pharisee known as Saul, he had been persecuting the Christian church, Jesus had appeared to him and confronted him with these words: "Saul, Saul! Why do you persecute me?" (Acts 9:4). Not "Why do you persecute my people?" but "Why do you persecute *me*?" The implication is clear. What you do to the church you do to Christ. If you oppose the church you oppose Christ. On another occasion Jesus said, "I tell you the truth, whatever you did for one of the least of these brothers of mine, you did for me" (Matt. 25:40). How we treat our brothers and sisters is how we treat Jesus.

In any church there will be some who have virtually nothing to do with the rest of that body of Christians. I'm not talking about visitors, or those whose main church is elsewhere but who come occasionally for a friendly catch-up, or the one or two who can't handle large crowds right now and so keep a very low profile on a Sunday, or those who are not yet

Christians but who come regularly and are still working their way through the claims of Christ.

I'm thinking of those who come regularly and think of this as their church, yet make minimal effort to get to know all the other people. At our own church, they are those who I have to race to the door just to greet before they disappear. Every church has them. You might even be one of them.

If that's you, then I can't stop you from behaving that way. But I can tell you that each week when you snub your church family, you are snubbing Jesus himself. You may be theologically sharp as a pin. You may be very disciplined in your devotional life. But if you are not interested in your church family, then your relationship with Jesus is very poor indeed. Your attitude to them is the true guide to your attitude to him. Ignore the church by all means, but please don't pretend you love Jesus.

Christ's bride

In fact, the church is Jesus' bride. Paul spells this out to his readers elsewhere. Writing to the church family in Corinth, he could say: "I am jealous for you with a godly jealousy. I promised you to one husband, to Christ, so that I might present you as a pure virgin to him" (2 Cor. 11:2).

Kevin DeYoung highlights an important implication of this:

Any husband worth the paper his marriage license is printed on will be jealous to guard the good name of his wife. . . . And woe to the friend who comes around your house, hangs out, and expects to have a good time, all the while getting digs in on your bride. Who wants a friend who rolls his eyes and sighs every time your wife walks into the room?

Apparently, some people imagine Jesus wants friends like that. They roll their eyes and sigh over the church.[5]

I was mulling this over recently on a long walk with a great friend of mine named Joe. He married a wonderful Christian girl a few years ago, and I asked him how it would have affected our friendship if I had taken no interest whatsoever in her—from the moment they started to get to know each other, right through their engagement and into their married life, for me not to have had any desire to get to know her, talk to her, or befriend her. Joe didn't need time to think about his answer: our friendship would not have remained at all close. She is his beloved. I could not have snubbed her and somehow hung in there with him as if nothing was amiss. It's obvious, really.

The church is Christ's bride, his beloved. Snub her, reject her, ignore her and it is hard to see how you are really going to get anywhere with him. What you think about his pride and joy says a lot about what you think of him. If these truths are in any way convicting you of the shallowness of your relationship with Christ and his bride, it is urgent that you do something about it. You need to love the church. If that feels like something that just doesn't come naturally to you, then pray for God to change your heart.

I should probably say something to those of us who are shy—those who *do* love the church and want to get to know her better, but who don't always find it easy getting to know others. It might be your temperament or it might be some very painful past experiences, but either way, putting yourself out there is at best draining and at worst a big fear for you. No doubt the rest of your church needs to raise their game and make more of an effort. But you probably need to pray about this. Ask God that your love for Christ would lead to such a love for his people that your interest in them would eclipse any natural fears and inhibitions.

It can be easy if we're naturally shy (and I include myself in this) to step back and wait for everyone else to approach us.

But not only is it their job to be interested in me; I need to be interested in them. You might be worried that you're just not an interesting enough person. Well, I'll let you into a great observation I heard a few years back: what makes someone interesting *to* others is that they are interested *in* others.

No church will always be easy to love. Which is why we need to look at the church theologically and not just humanly.

Christians need to love the church. Any local church will have its idiosyncrasies and its foibles. No church will always be easy to love. Which is why we need to look at the church theologically and not just humanly. The church is a body—the body of Christ—and indeed the bride of Christ.

One of the ways in which we love the church is by keeping in mind the way in which it is grounded in the Trinity. The unity in diversity of the church reflects the unity in diversity of the Godhead. It is a perspective that will help us to cherish our diversity while functioning together as a single entity.

THE CHURCH'S WITNESS

The night before he died, Jesus spent time with his disciples, preparing them for life without him. A good deal of this preparation was taken up with a prayer Jesus prayed in his disciples' hearing. That he intended them to listen in suggests there was much that they—and we—scould learn from it.

In the course of his prayer, Jesus prays for the disciples gathered around him. He also prays for future disciples—those later generations of followers who will come to believe in his name through the ministry of these first believers. It is a prayer for all Christians through subsequent centuries of history, including us. This is Jesus praying for you! If you ever wondered what his priorities for your life might be, here's a good place to look:

> I pray also for those who will believe in me through their [the first apostles'] message, that all of them may be one, Father, just as you are in me and I am in you. May they also be in us so that the world may believe that you have sent me. I have given them the glory that you gave me, that they may be one as we are one: I in them and you in me. May they be brought to complete unity to let the world know that you sent me and have loved them even as you have loved me. (John 17:20–23)

Jesus prays for our unity, the very unity he has already been talking about: unity grounded in the Trinity. The unity we are to have as believers is the unity enjoyed by God the Father and God the Son. It reminds us that the unity of the church is not institutional, not man-made. It is unity in the truth of the message Jesus came to teach, unity that comes as we are brought into relationship with God the Trinity. We get to join in the oneness of God!

And it is a unity that is going to have a significant impact. It will cause the world to believe two amazing truths: that the Father has sent the Son and that we have received the same love from the Father that the Son has. It is a unity that transcends all other earthly considerations: politics, ethnicity, social background, level of education, wealth, and culture.

Neptune was the first planet to be discovered by mathematics rather than by observation. It wasn't that someone chanced upon it while looking through a telescope one day, but that they had worked out that it must exist and even where it would be. I'm told the clever chap in question was John Couch Adams during the 1840s. He and others had noticed various irregularities in the orbit of Uranus. It deviated significantly from its expected path. The only explanation was that there was something else out there, some other planetary body whose gravity was tugging away at it and causing it to move out of its predicted orbit. Individuals like Adams were able to extrapolate from these irregularities exactly where this other planet must be. None of them ever needed to have seen it. The existence and location of Neptune was a mathematical certainty before they ever set eyes on it.

We've seen that the church is to be marked by the unity of God the Trinity. Our life together is to reflect that same love, mutual delight, and other-person-centeredness that characterizes the relationships of the Father, Son, and Spirit. And as the world looks on, it will see what appear to be all sorts of irregularities, deviations from the normal paths of behavior: Christians showing unworldly care and concern for one another. Hearts, wallets, and homes cheerfully opened to help those in need. Those from backgrounds you wouldn't normally see together enjoying their unity in Christ. Believers very different from one another but lit by a love of meeting together, of praising their Savior and taking his word to heart.

All these things should be deeply curious irregularities to a watching world—lines of behavior that do not move in the directions people have come to expect. An orbit of life that is unmistakably different. Instances of deep love that indicate beyond doubt the gravitational pull of a greater and unseen presence. An undeniable sign that this community of believers is being held together by nothing less than a love that is divine in origin. The spectator who begins to extrapolate from these earth-bound irregularities will, in the end, be directed to the perfect heavenly analogue of them all.

The only explanation for a church like this can be, ultimately, the reality of God the Trinity.

8

WHAT REALLY HAPPENS WHEN YOU TALK TO GOD

The Trinity and Prayer

THERE ARE TIMES in life when we need help to speak.

In the 2004 presidential election campaign, there was some speculation at one point as to whether George W. Bush was being fed lines during his televised debate with Senator John Kerry. There were, supposedly, telltale pauses before he gave each of his answers, and some suggested that the shirt collar and the tuft of hair around his ear could have easily concealed a small earpiece. I don't think the speculation came to much, and evidently it didn't affect the outcome of the campaign. But it is not hard to imagine why someone in that situation would have valued a little outside help. In the cut and thrust of an unscripted, live debate, we would probably need all the help we could get.

Or think about the movies. It has become a staple now in rom-coms: the leading man is a bit of a bumbling drip, bless him.[1] At some point he is going to have to bite the bullet and declare his feelings to the girl of his dreams. And so his buddies need to help him out. They tell him in advance what to say and make him jot it down,[2] or else while he is outside the house calling up to her at her window they hide around the corner and whisper him some lines.[3]

As a pastor, I have times when I need to have a difficult conversation with someone. I'm not at my best in these situations, especially when there might be the potential for conflict or strong emotions. At the very moment when I need it the most, my mind will go blank, and I won't know what to say. So I think about what might need to be said in advance and then spend some time trying to work out how best to say it. I'll even write some notes to try to get it all clear in my head.

So there are times in life when we need a little help to speak. And every time we pray is one of those times.

The difficulty of prayer

Prayer can often feel like one of those difficult conversations. It is a simple act: talking to God. But it is also a spiritual act. It is not just any conversation with any person. We are addressing the living God. And that requires some help.

Prayer is hard. C. S. Lewis described it in the following way, and I'm so grateful that he did. It means I'm not the only one who finds it difficult.

> Well, let's now at any rate come clean. Prayer is irksome. An excuse to omit it is never unwelcome. When it is over, this casts a feeling of relief and holiday over the rest of the day. We are reluctant to begin. We are delighted to finish. While we are at prayer, but not while we are reading a novel or solving a cross-word puzzle, any trifle is enough to distract us.[4]

Looking for help

Many of us instinctively look for help in certain places. We look to some of the great examples of prayer. We read the biography of a George Müller or a Hudson Taylor and feel inspired by the spectacular answers to prayer they experienced. Or we look at our technique in prayer and at how some adjustments to that might help us pray more effectively. We rethink how and when we pray and start making some new resolutions, determining that if we pray instead at *this* time of day in *this* way using *this* new format, it will all get going. My prayer life will take off.

Both things can often help, but it is interesting to see that neither is where the Bible takes us. Scripture is not technique but theology. Learning from godly models and thinking through the practicalities all have their place, but first and foremost we need to be reminded of what God is like. Prayer takes its cue not so much from what we do but from who God is. A failure to pray is often a failure to grasp who God truly is. To be clear on prayer, we need to be clear on him.

Which brings us to the Trinity.

Understanding the Trinity sheds light on what's been going on every time we've prayed. Whether we are conscious of it or not, Christian prayer is trinitarian. When we come to God in prayer we are, in fact, engaging with the Trinity. Let's listen to Paul: "Through him [Jesus] we . . . have access to the Father by one Spirit" (Eph. 2:18).

This is how we relate to God. This is what is going on when we pray. Christian prayer is trinitarian because it is offered by the Spirit, through the Son, to the Father.

BY THE SPIRIT

No Christian prayer happens apart from the Holy Spirit. He is at work not just as we pray, but even beforehand, prompting us to pray in the first place.

The Spirit and why we pray

As Christians, we enjoy the gift of God's presence in our lives. We are not on our own, attempting to follow Christ through our own strength and wisdom. God has come to dwell within us. We have received the Holy Spirit. Understanding this truth and the difference it makes is crucial in living the Christian life, and this is the concern of Paul in Romans 8.

But as well as understanding the Spirit's work, we need to understand his character. Actually, the two are linked. As we come to know the kind of Spirit we have received, we are better able to go with the grain of his work in our lives. See this connection in the following passage:

> If by the Spirit you put to death the misdeeds of the body, you will live, because those who are led by the Spirit of God are sons of God. For you did not receive a spirit that makes you a slave again to fear, but you received the Spirit of sonship. And by him we cry, "*Abba*, Father." (Rom. 8:13–15)

Paul is concerned that his readers will know what this Spirit is like. If they do not, they will not properly understand his work.

Making his presence felt

Some people have an unmistakable presence. The moment they enter the room, the whole room knows. They fill every room they step into. I think of a dear friend and colleague of mine, big of build and bigger of personality. You can't miss him. Stealth is not one of his capabilities. If he's anywhere within a half-mile radius, you will know about it.

The Spirit has an unmistakable presence too. We need to get this right: the Spirit is not one who makes us a "slave again to fear." That's not the kind of Spirit we have received. The effect of his presence is not that we experience unremitting fear of God's judgment. That would have been an appropriate posture toward God before we came to Christ. But through Christ we have been justified and forgiven, and so the Spirit comes as a Spirit of sonship. Through him we receive a growing sense of our sonship before God and of his father-hood to us. And so our posture toward God changes accordingly. Instead of fear, we can have confidence.

This is why the gospel is so wonderful! We are not just pardoned as sinners but adopted as sons. Pardon alone would remove our condemnation, but it would bring us no closer to friendship with God. A convicted murderer who receives a presidential pardon would have no grounds to think he can now pop around to the White House whenever he likes.[5] Pardon alone would not bring us into the arms of God.

Knowing our sonship

But, through Christ, we have received far more than a pardon. By faith we are united to him, and, just as the union of a marriage leads to the sharing of assets, so too our faith union with Christ enables not just our condemnation to be borne by him, but his perfect righteousness to be credited to us. More than that, our union is also filial: Jesus becomes our older brother and we share in his sonship before the Father.

The role of the Spirit is to massage these truths into our hearts. God has chosen us not only to be spared the condemna-tion that our sins deserve, but also to be part of his family. We can bask in his affection and grace. There is even a wonderful inheritance to look forward to. And so, as we come to the Father, the Spirit prompts us to cry out, "*Abba*, Father."

Abba. Don't think Swedish glam-rock and brightly colored spandex. For Jesus and his contemporaries, "Abba" was what you would call your dad. It was homely, intimate, and familial.

And it now characterizes how we are to approach God. He is not the unknowable "other," still less a finger-wagging authority figure, but our Father: "By him we cry '*Abba*, Father.' The Spirit himself testifies with our spirit that we are God's children" (Rom. 8:15–16).

Two things are mentioned here:

- The Spirit moves us to call out to God as our Father.
- The Spirit bears witness to us that we are God's children.

I suspect this is one activity, not two. As we call God *Father*, the Spirit testifies to our inner being that we are indeed God's children. The act of prayer reminds us that we are on praying terms with God our Father.

If this is right, then prayer itself is a means of assurance. As we avail ourselves of the privilege of addressing God as *Father*, we are becoming more deeply conscious of the utter appropriateness of doing so as his adopted children. Prayer is essentially evangelical—as we pray we are reenacting the gospel to ourselves.

The Spirit and what we pray

But the Spirit doesn't just start us off in prayer and then leave us to it. He is right in there with us, helping us as we pray.

A while ago someone at an inquirers' course asked me a good question: What does it feel like to be a Christian?

I wasn't entirely sure where to start. No one had asked me this before. So I said what I always say when I don't know what to say, "Let's open this up for discussion and see what others think," and hoped one of the other Christians in the room might have a punt at it.

I'm not sure what the "right" answer is, but something of authentic Christian experience is captured for us by Paul in Romans 8. Two things are true of us as Christians:

- We have been adopted as sons (v. 16).
- We await our full adoption as sons (v. 23).

This is it. As Christians we are caught between these two realities, knowing we have been given something in Christ—being able to taste something of it—but not yet being able to enjoy it fully. There is wonder at what we have, but also a yearning for what we're waiting for.

Praying when we don't know what to pray for

This means we are often weak. The tension of living with what we have and don't yet have, the pain of living as new creations in the old order of things, can leave us disoriented. We don't always know the way forward. We don't always know what to be praying for. Paul says as much: "The Spirit helps us in our weakness. We do not know what we ought to pray for, but the Spirit himself intercedes for us with groans that words cannot express" (Rom. 8:26).

Someone dear to us is afflicted. Do we pray for deliverance or endurance? Or a bit of both? Sometimes we don't know where to start or what is best. A friend in the middle of a very messy crisis expressed his bewilderment candidly: "I don't know God's way through this!" He didn't, and often we don't either.

On our own we are very weak. But the whole point is that we do not pray on our own. The Spirit intercedes for us. He does not "take over" and pray instead of us, shoving us out of the way so he can do it "properly" without us. He assists us. As we pray, he prays.

Think of a dad teaching his son to swing a golf club. The father will not make his son stand off to the side just to watch and take notes. He will stand over his boy, putting his own hands over his son's, fixing his grip, so that the two of them—together—swing the club. You wouldn't be able to say which of them actually played the shot; they both did.

The Spirit partners with us as we pray. And as he prays, he does so in a particular way: "The Spirit intercedes for the saints in accordance with God's will" (Rom. 8:27).

Praying in line with God's will

The Spirit prays "in accordance with God's will." He is able to take our weak prayers and point them in the right direction, to swing the club with us, so that despite our weak grip and poor aim the ball leaves the tee and finds its intended target. Our prayers, muddled in our own minds as we pray them, reach the Father in such a way that they are in accordance with his will.

Just think about that. It is wonderful. It means that no matter how weak and bewildered we might feel, the Spirit intercedes with us and for us and enables our prayers to honor God and hit the right spot. It means that no prayer is a wasted prayer.

Because he is Trinity, God prays with us as we pray to him.

We are not left to speak on our own. The Spirit helps us. He prompts us and then prays with us. His presence is critical for both the prompting and the content of our prayers.

Put another way, God is involved at both ends of our prayers—not just the receiving of them but also the offering of them too. Every prayer we have prayed as Christians has been not just to God, but from and by him. C. S. Lewis has called prayer a divine "soliloquy"[6]—God talking to himself through us. That takes it a bit too far, as though we were entirely incidental to the process, but it is a great reminder of something we are often unaware of: because he is Trinity, God prays with us as we pray to him.

THROUGH THE SON

One of the great things about being a pastor is that occasionally I get to visit the workplaces of church members. Sometimes it's to meet colleagues with whom they have been sharing their faith so that I can field questions. Sometimes it is to satisfy my own curiosity about what their work life is like. Sometimes it is just an opportunity to hang out with them and get a feel for what their life involves once they've left the spiritual decompression chamber that is our church foyer. I've visited hospitals, offices, schools, prisons, and, once, an air traffic control tower.

Once I got to visit a gas processing plant. Maybe not as exciting as an air traffic control tower or as edgy as a prison, but a day to remember nonetheless. The guy I was shadowing was high up in his company. Every now and then he would drop in on a plant to assess what was going on and provide support to the plant-management types. It was on one of these jaunts that he invited me to join him. It meant having to get up hours before dawn. But on the plus side, the plant was on the coast and near a beautiful national park. Keith said he had been there before and promised me lunch at a great seafood restaurant the company had an account with.

I wasn't quite sure what to expect. Gas processing plants, with all their gantries, pipes, and tanks, tend to be where showdowns take place at the end of thrillers. Lots of places for tense shoot-outs and things that will explode lavishly if hit by stray gunfire. So I half expected to see Jack Bauer run past as bullets ricocheted overhead. But instead we spent most of the day sitting in offices.

However, what made it such a memorable day was not the surroundings but the level of kudos I enjoyed because of my link to Keith. He'd made it clear to the staff that I was his guest for the day and that I was to be accorded every courtesy that applied to him. Which turned out to be a big deal.

I know nothing about gas processing. I didn't even know that gas *needed* processing. I just assumed they piped it straight into my home from the inside of a mountain somewhere. And yet here I was being treated like a senior executive. People who earn far more than I ever will, and who no doubt had worked hard to reach their position, were rushing around making sure I had everything I needed. They were tripping over themselves to make me comfortable and even explaining, with endless patience, what this whole plant was for in the first place. I'm sure they had far better things to do, but that day they were happy to bend over backward to accommodate someone who had no obvious business being in their world.

All of that was because of one thing. Keith had said to them, "He's with me." That changed everything. Without that status I could not have got past the front gate, let alone the room where they give out the yellow hard hats. But *with* that status I could go straight in at his level.

We have already seen that the deepest, strongest, and most exquisitely happy relationship in all the universe exists within the Godhead. Listen again to the music that exists between the Father and the Son:

> I do as the Father has commanded me, so that the world may know that I love the Father. (John 14:31, ESV)

The Father loves the Son and has placed everything in his hands. (John 3:35)

This is my Son, whom I love. (Mark 9:7)

The mission of Jesus, as we have seen, has been to open that relationship up to us. By his life, death, and resurrection he has secured our forgiveness and adoption. We're with him now. And that means we get to go straight in at his level.

It makes such a difference to prayer to keep this in our own heads.

The party has already begun

Prayer can often seem like we have to drum up a rapport with God. It can feel forced and awkward, as though we both know I have no real business being there. It's a little like a chance meeting with a great dignitary whom you really admire but have never met before. All pleasantries but no real dynamic. We're starting from scratch.

But the reality of prayer is very different. For a start, we have, in Christ, every business being there. We are joined to him. He calls us his "friends" (John 15:14). And so there is no ice to break. His Father has been expecting us. The invitation to come was from him in the first place. The rapport already exists between the Father and Son, and through our union with Jesus we become part of that rapport. We are being encouraged to join in, not to establish an easy dynamic but to join the one that already exists. We go straight in at Jesus' level. We are loved by his Father with the same love that Jesus has enjoyed for eternity (John 17:23). As Fred Sanders puts it, "If you have ever become weary of working up the right response in prayer or worship, you can glimpse the relief of being able to approach prayer and worship with the knowledge that the party already started before you arrived."[7]

We pray through the Son. This is why Jesus encourages us to pray in his name.

Praying in Jesus' name

"I tell you the truth, my Father will give you whatever you ask in my name. . . . Ask and you will receive, and your joy will be complete" (John 16:23–24).

We do not approach the Father in our own name. That would be to come to him on the basis of who we are by ourselves and on our own merits. Jesus invites us to come in through our connection to him.

This is not to suggest that his name is a magic formula or secret password. It is not like a special promotional number we have to enter in order to get a special deal. Jesus is not saying that every prayer which concludes with the formula "in Jesus' name" will be answered, whereas every prayer that does not will immediately slam into the ceiling.

The key is to understand what Jesus means by his name. It is not just a label. His name involves his identity and character. Praying in his name is not hacking into his spiritual email account and firing off messages, but lining ourselves up with who he is and what he stands for. It is to share his priorities and concerns, to pray in the light of his agenda, not ours.

If we ignore this, we will just think of verses like those above as spiritual blank checks. If I pray for a Porsche in his name, then I will definitely get a Porsche. Jesus is not saying that. Prayer is not room service. When he invites us to pray in his name, Jesus is highlighting the efficacy of prayer when it is consistent with his character—such prayer will be granted. The more we know him and what he loves, the more we get into what he is into and allow that to shape our praying, the more we will see our prayers being answered. We will truly be praying in his name.

Remembering the basis of prayer

As we pray to the Father through the Son we are reminding ourselves that we come only through the merits and standing of Jesus. It is not about any merit or standing I have managed to accrue. I might have had a winner of a day as a Christian, a day conscious of the Lord's good presence, of joyfully walking in his ways, of opportunities for doing good taken and temptation resisted. It is easy to think that at the end of a day like that I can swagger into God's presence like a conquering hero.

But I might instead have had an awful day as a Christian—a day when I was not mindful of God's presence, a day focused on me and my wants, a day of good opportunities squandered and bad ones taken. The kind of day that makes you wonder if God ever thinks about quitting as God. After a day like that, we won't feel quite so compelled to pray. It'll be a long while before we feel we can look God in the eye again.

In each case I am basing my standing before God on my spiritual performance. I am coming to God in my name. And I want (need!) that name to look as buffed and shiny as possible for God to accept it.

It amazes me how quickly I slide into this kind of thinking. It is a hopeless way to approach prayer. For starters, none of us is great at evaluating how "Christian" our day has been. We are conscious of only some of our sin, and much of it we don't even notice. There are also times, I suspect, when we are more honoring to God than we realize; when we are used by him in ways we didn't even know about; when, deep down, our hearts really were longing for his ways and not just our own. We ourselves don't have the best measure of how we're doing.

But far more importantly, if I am thinking this way I am forgetting the whole basis of prayer. I am coming to the Father through my spiritual labors rather than through Jesus. It would be like my driving up to the gas processing plant and announcing that in my final chemistry exam at school I got 11% and that I was now ready to be let in for some seafood lunch.

It is not about what I can do but about what Jesus has done. As Ron Dunn has said, when we come before God, the throne room is sprinkled "not with the sweat of my good works, but with the blood of his sacrifice."[8]

We pray through the Son.

TO THE FATHER

On one occasion, Jesus' followers asked for some lessons on prayer. By all accounts it was what John the Baptist was doing with his disciples; Jesus' disciples had caught wind of this and may have felt they were missing out. Jesus' first response was to teach them to pray to the Father: "When you pray, say: 'Father . . .'" (Luke 11:2).

We are to direct our prayers to the Father.

Prayer to the Son? Prayer to the Spirit?

Now that raises a couple of questions right off the bat: What about praying to Jesus? Or to the Spirit? Are we supposed to pray only to God the Father?

The norm in Scripture, in the teaching of both Jesus and his apostles, is for prayer to be directed to God the Father. Jesus' teaching for his disciples—what we have come to call the Lord's Prayer—is programmatic. We pray to "our Father in heaven."

Though this is the norm, there are some examples in the New Testament of people praying directly to Jesus. Just before he was killed, Stephen prayed, "Lord Jesus, receive my Spirit" (Acts 7:59). The Bible ends with a prayer to Jesus, as John writes, "Amen. Come, Lord Jesus" (Rev. 22:20). It is clearly not wrong to pray to Jesus! Indeed, there are times when, as we reflect on the depth of his love for us in going to the cross, it is hard not to pray to him in worship, thanks, and adoration. This is entirely right. But, given that Jesus himself encourages us to pray to the Father, we would not be honoring Jesus if we prayed only to him.

There are no examples in the Bible of people praying to the Spirit. But it would not be wrong. The Spirit is as much divine and personal as the Father and the Son, and our relationship with him is just as personal as it is with them. However, the lack of biblical examples for doing so must caution us against ever insisting on it or making it our normal practice. The Spirit is, after all, rooting for us in our efforts to pray to the Father, prompting, equipping, and even praying with us as we do so. I suspect, on the whole, he would rather we pray by him than to him.

So the biblical pattern for normal prayer is that it is directed to the Father.

Not muddling up the persons of the Trinity

Another comment needs to be made. In our praying we need to be conscious of the persons of the Trinity, careful not to muddle them up. In some ways I am hesitant to say this because it might sound like we need someone to theologically spell-check our prayers before we hit the "send" button. But we do not honor the Father by speaking to him as though he were the Son. And yet it is quite common to hear Christians of some maturity addressing the Father and, say, thanking him for his death on the cross.

I work with two fellow pastors, Will and Andy. For the

record, we look nothing alike. At the end of a recent church meeting, after which Will had preached his heart out, someone on their way out passed me and said, "Andy, thank you for that sermon!" I didn't really know what to say (other than, perhaps, "How many mistakes can you make in just one comment?!"), so I ended up thanking them and passing on their gratitude to the relevant person.

This kind of thing happens more often than you might think. (My stock answer now when someone thanks me for a sermon I didn't preach is simply to say, "It was no trouble," which at least is true.) Now, this is not something I lie awake worrying about, and it's not exactly grounds for church discipline. But it does suggest a lack of attention to who is actually doing what and a possibility that in people's eyes we might not actually be three separate people but just "the clergy."

But I think it does matter with God. Remember, the Trinity is made up not of persons A, B, and C, but of Father, Son, and Spirit. They are not interchangeable. To imply otherwise in the way we pray is to risk dishonoring the persons of the Trinity and the distinct roles they have played in our salvation.

Hours before his death, Jesus was in torment in the garden of Gethsemane. The full weight of what was about to happen was upon him. The prospect of the death that awaited him was unbearable. He prayed with desperate longing not to have to face it, not to have to drink that cup for us. And yet, deep though that distress was—unimaginable to us—there was another desire within him that was deeper still: for the Father's will to be done in his life. And so the final, ultimate prayer in that evening of turmoil was not "Take this cup," but "Do your will." To the end, that was Jesus' greatest resolution: to please and follow his Father and, by doing so, to serve and save us.

In light of all that, do we honor the Son and all that he

endured for us when we pray, "Father, we thank you for dying for us?" I suspect not.

When Jesus taught his followers to pray, he wanted them to know exactly what his Father was like.

What the Father is like

Accessible

It is easy to think of God as being remote, distant, and uninvolved. For many, that might be their own experience with their fathers—the guy behind the sports section who occasionally writes a check. Maybe we even think God the Father sent the Son precisely so that he didn't have to deal with us directly himself. The Son is interested and involved, the Father aloof and disinterested. We could not be more wrong.

> Ask and it will be given to you; seek and you will find; knock and the door will be opened to you. For everyone who asks receives; he who seeks finds; and to him who knocks, the door will be opened. (Matt. 7:7–8)

God is interested. God is *there*. He made us, knows us, and cares deeply about us. He is not just theoretically around, like the friend who says you can call him any time but never actually answers the phone. We have access to God. Jesus has secured it.

And it is ongoing. Jesus is encouraging us to be persistent in coming to the Father. He uses the present tense—we are to *keep on* asking, seeking, knocking. It is an ongoing activity, not something we do once and then don't ever have to do again. We are in constant need of the Father's help and so we are to come to him continually. More to the point, we *can* keep coming.

British evangelist Rico Tice likens this situation to a

well-known photograph of President John F. Kennedy. In the picture, Kennedy is seated at the Resolute desk in the Oval Office working away at a pile of papers before him. Underneath the desk we see his little son John-John poking his head out and looking up at the camera. It is a wonderful image. This is one of the most protected rooms in the world. You don't just get to wander in and say "Hi." There are multiple layers of security and protocol. And yet little John-John can toddle in with his toys, sit under his daddy's desk, and play on the floor. He might be everyone else's president, but to this boy he is Dad. It is a picture of access and familiarity even before the most powerful man in the world.

I keep a copy of that picture on the wall of my office to remind me that this is the kind of access we now enjoy with God. He is the great Sovereign Lord and yet also our Father. The moment we knock he will answer. We want to seek him out and we'll find him. No question. We ask and he will give without blinking. Our Father is accessible.

Good

This access would not be of much value were God not also good. And so to underline the point, Jesus gets all the dads listening to him to think about how they respond when their kids need something. "Which of you, if his son asks for bread, will give him a stone? Or if he asks for a fish, will give him a snake?" (Matt. 7:9–10).

One imagines that Jesus' question was met by silence. No dad would think of behaving that way. It is an absurd picture. Bread and fish were the staple foodstuffs then. Just imagine a hungry boy coming up to his father and asking for either. His dad smiles down at his boy and says, "Of course, son. Hold out your hands and close your eyes." As the child holds out his hands he feels a lump of something heavy. Mouth salivating, he puts it in his mouth and bites down hard on it. And breaks several teeth. Or he feels something scaly and lifts it expectantly to his mouth, only to discover it is still moving and sinking poisonous teeth into him.

It's not what decent dads do. It's not even what the pretty mediocre ones do. And that's the kicker: "If you, then, though you are evil, know how to give good gifts to your children, how much more will your Father in heaven give good gifts to those who ask him!" (Matt. 7:11).

Even dopey human fathers have figured out how to give basic good things to their kids. Do we think God is any less of a Father than that? Isn't there just the slightest possibility that he's actually a *better* dad than that?

Defining fatherhood

We need to remember that God is the one who invented fatherhood. It's not that there is a human thing called fatherhood, and God then decides he's going to use that as his template of how to be a good God to us—human fatherhood being the real thing and God kind of ripping it off. No, there has always been fatherhood within the Trinity. We've seen that God the Father's fatherhood of God the Son has existed for all eternity. God defines fatherhood, and human fatherhood is but a faint reflection.

This may be why Jesus slips in that aside about the dads in his audience being evil. It is a given. It's what we humans are like, even those of us who know how to give good things to our kids.

I'm sure there will be many reading this book who have unhappy associations with their fathers. Some will never have known a dad, some are grieving for him, while others are struggling to forgive him. Many others of us have had great dads and we thank God for them. But even the very best human dads are a pale reflection of the perfect Father we have in heaven: "How much more will your Father in heaven give good gifts to those who ask him!"

This is the Father we pray to. He is not begrudging or reluctant. He loves giving good things. He gets a kick out of it. He won't always give us what we want, and we don't always know what is truly going to be good for us. There may be times when, for the sake of what is good for us, God doesn't give us what we ask for. But we can be sure of one thing: he is more ready to hear and answer our prayers than we are to offer them.

Understanding the Trinity helps us to lift up the hood to see what is going on when we pray. And what it shows us is incredible. Words you and I might mutter Godward at the end of a tiring day are not just floating out into the ether and struggling to find the way to their intended target. The concept that we can talk to God is in itself something to wonder at. But it is even more wonderful to think that, by talking to him, we are entering into the dynamic of the Trinity itself. God has opened up his own inner relationships and granted us access. Prayer involves our coming to our eager Father, spiritually piggybacking on his perfect Son as we make our request, and all by the power of his Holy Spirit.

9

TO THE PRAISE OF FATHER, SON, AND HOLY SPIRIT

The Trinity and Worship

IT WAS A BIT OF a disappointment.

The Aletsch Glacier is one of the most famous sites in the Swiss Alps—unmissable, everyone had said. But once we'd peeled ourselves from our coach seats and attempted to straighten our legs after the long journey, it looked like just a blob of ice on a mountain. We'd travelled for hours along twisting mountain roads, cramped into seats so small we could have licked our kneecaps. And now, finally disgorged onto the viewing platform and learning to walk again, we wondered if any of this was really worth it.

It was only once we got a little closer that this feeling changed. We picked our way down a rocky path to a lower viewing point, one from which we could better see the detail of the surroundings, and for the first time we got a sense of its scale. I could now see why it is so famous.

For a start, it is *huge*. This is the largest glacier in the Alps. You could park my home town of Maidenhead on it and still have plenty of room around the edges. But it was only when we got up close that I got a true sense of its scale.

Recovering the scale of the gospel

Paul is on a mission to do a similar thing with our view of God. And I can think of no better way of closing this book than to see, through his eyes, the wonder of the love of God the Trinity.

In Ephesians 1:3–14, Paul takes us right up close so that we can begin to see the true dimensions of it all. It's a sense of scale we all need. I know, in my case, that unless Scripture regularly adjusts it, my view of God can easily begin to shrink, even to the point where I can think I'm doing him a favor by believing in him.

And so Paul lays before us something of the scale of what God has done for us. There is no lengthy introduction. He doesn't try to warm us up first. He takes his point and gets in our face with it: "Praise be to the God and Father of our Lord Jesus Christ, who has blessed us in the heavenly realms with every spiritual blessing in Christ" (v. 3).

Unless Scripture regularly adjusts it, my view of God can easily begin to shrink, even to the point where I can think I'm doing him a favor by believing in him.

God is to be praised. Not the forced praise that is the stock-in-trade for your standard paranoid dictator. Not a token or begrudging praise, which you don't mean but think might keep God on your side. No, the deserved and full-throated praise that is the natural response to all that God is and has done.

God has blessed us. It takes Paul just one verse to state. But it takes the next dozen verses to begin to unpack. It will take the rest of our lives to grasp and explore: God the Trinity has blessed us. And that's huge too.

Now, this might not send an immediate shiver down our spines. A sneezing fit in my office the other day triggered a hail of "bless you"s from colleagues in the next room. Saying "bless you" is a nice gesture. But God's blessing is much more than a sentiment. God, we've just been told, has blessed us with "every spiritual blessing in Christ."

Again, that might not grab us. "Spiritual blessing" sounds a little intangible. It feels a little like those alternative presents people seem to like giving at Christmas: having a distant star named after you or being given a few acres on the surface of Jupiter—theoretically nice, but hardly something we can get our hands on.

It helps to realize that, by spiritual blessings, Paul means blessings that come to us by the Holy Spirit. We can then begin to see what is going on. God the Father has blessed us, blessed us with everything in Jesus that's available. He's cleaned out the cupboard. And these blessings have come to us by the Holy Spirit.

To put it another way, God the Trinity has blessed us.

This becomes clear as Paul goes on. This passage is one long sentence in the original Greek that Paul wrote. Our English translations have broken it up into several sentences—people would pass out reading it aloud otherwise—but in reality it is one long exclamation. Paul can't contain himself. As he shows us these blessings he is like a young child trying to show us all his new toys at once: "There's *this*, and *this*—and come and look at *this!*" There is wonder and excitement as each phrase tumbles out over the next: "Look at what God the Trinity has done for us!"

But it is not some random splurge. As Paul goes through these blessings, he moves from what we have from the Father

(vv. 3–6) to what we have from the Son (vv. 7–12) and then from the Spirit (vv. 13–14). And as he rounds off what each person of the Godhead has done, he reminds us that all this is to issue forth in worship.

> to the praise of his glorious grace. (v. 6)
> for the praise of his glory. (v. 12)
> to the praise of his glory. (v. 14)

In other words, the work of each person of the Trinity is a reason to give God praise and adoration.

CHOSEN BY THE FATHER

He chose us in Christ (v. 4).

God always makes the first move. He initiates relationship with us, not vice versa. We see this again and again in the Bible. I can't think of a single example of someone initiating a relationship with God. He chooses us.

It might be that some of us came to faith in Christ at a particular moment in our lives. We might even be able to point to the date or time we became a Christian. In my case, I can pin it down to a summer's afternoon in August 1993. I was on a week away with a church youth group. Over the previous couple of months I had been drawn to the teachings of Jesus. I was becoming more and more convinced that he was who he claimed to be. But that August afternoon was the first time I realized that I consciously needed to make a response to Christ. If he had given his life for me, I reasoned, then I needed to give my life to him. Anything less would not truly reflect who he was. That day I "chose Christ." It was real. But looking back through the lens of Ephesians 1, I could only have chosen Christ because the Father had first chosen me.

It is the same for all of us, whatever our story. We are Christians today because the Father chose us in Christ.

Why

Paul shows us why we were chosen: "to be holy and blameless in his sight" (v. 4).

God chose us because he wanted to be able to see us as holy and blameless. Think about what that implies.

I have a love-hate relationship with those people with clipboards who hang around shopping malls to question members of the public. I'm never in the mood to be stopped. When I see one of them bearing down on me I tend to swerve evasively, even if it lands me in a shop which I would normally never think of entering.

But I also don't like *not* being approached. After all, my thoughts and opinions are critically important to society. Frankly, they should be lining up to survey me.

One day I saw one such survey-taker observing the crowds passing and waiting for the right sort of person to stop and question. As he saw me, he immediately started his approach. On this particular occasion I wanted to reward his discernment, so I stopped. His opening question: "Good morning, sir! Would you be interested in having plastic surgery?"

He'd chosen me all right, but it wasn't flattering.

God's choice of us is humbling. He didn't choose us because we are impressive individuals or because he thought we'd be indispensable players on his team. Quite the opposite. He chose us because, left to our own devices, we are unholy and blameworthy.

When

Paul also shows us when we were chosen: "He chose us in [Christ] before the creation of the world" (v. 4).

This is astonishing. There was a time before this world existed. Before anything existed. And in that pre-creation time God did something: he determined that we would be his. That we would come to him in Christ.

This can sometimes make people uncomfortable. Is God being fair to choose us in this way? Isn't it all rather arbitrary? Does it mean there are people he *hasn't* chosen? How does that fit in with his being loving?

These are good questions, and there is a place for them. But the danger in being caught up in what we're not being told (in this passage, at least) is that we miss the beauty of what we *are* being told.

God is in control. Not just of creation—we probably already knew that—but of our salvation. It is entirely in his hands. It wasn't cooked up on the fly as God ran around responding to the mess of human sin. Nor is it the case that our future destiny had been hanging in the balance until, moments before our conversion, God finally swung in our favor. It was all planned before the creation of the world. It is not contingent on anything in this world. This is incredibly reassuring.

I was recently invited by some friends to join their spinning class. In my mind floated images of kindly grannies and cotton looms. The reality was a sweaty room, bright lights, thumping music, lots of exercise bikes, people in spandex looking far too happy to be there, and about an hour of pain. It was my latest scheme to shed some pounds and get in approximate shape. The advantage of this class was that friends were involved and there would be hefty penalties if I didn't show up. And yet I can already feel the attraction of dropping out. I'm never in the mood to go and, even when I'm there, all I can think about is stopping. It's hard work.

The Christian life can feel similarly fraught with the temptation to throw in the towel. We can imagine any number of ways in which we might give up our walk with Christ. We are conscious of our spiritual weaknesses: we might buckle under the pressure of opposition, we might get taken for a ride theologically by some plausible-sounding but misleading teaching, there might be some whopper of a temptation just around the corner that'll floor us. In ourselves we are weak and we often feel it.

When we're battling to keep going, it's a great comfort to know that we have been chosen—even before the creation of the world. Before we knew what we were about, before we ever needed changing, before matter existed, before space and time and physics, the Father had us in mind and determined that we were to be his. What a wonderful truth!

This is all for the praise of his glorious grace. His choice of us is to prompt our worship of him. I am to adore the Father for his free, undeserved, and remarkable choosing of even me to be one of his people.

RESCUED BY THE SON

A mere glance through Ephesians 1:3–14 shows us Paul's emphasis. In this one (admittedly long) sentence he mentions Christ fifteen times and being "in Christ" eleven times. We can't possibly miss Jesus.

One of my earliest memories is of a family vacation in southern England. I was at that age boys reach when we discover a whole new gear in our locomotive capabilities, a stage when we're done with walking. We now know what our legs can do, and if we're going anywhere, we're *running* there.

My family were staying in a hotel with a large garden. Something at the far end of the garden had evidently caught my attention, because on this occasion I was steaming across the lawn at full speed. So single-minded was I in my determination to achieve warp speed while running that I was undeterred by the presence of a large swimming pool across my path. In fact, I attempted to run straight across it. Onlookers later commented that my legs were running in midair for a few micro-moments—like someone from a Looney Tunes cartoon—before gravity finally won over and I plunged down into the water.

Fortunately my father was nearby and immediately dived in and fished me out. I can well imagine the heroic swagger with which he carried me back, fresh from near death, to where the rest of the family were sitting. He presented me—dripping wet but manifestly alive—to my mother, who promptly told him off for letting me get that close to the pool in the first place.

Many people have a story like that. At any given moment, up and down the land, hapless toddlers are being plucked from danger by their parents as they wander toward peril, oblivious to its threat. Fast-moving traffic, open fires, raging torrents, cliff edges, exposed electrical sockets, oncoming aircraft. Some of us will have been rescued numerous times during the course of our childhood.

But the biggest rescue of all has come through God the Son: "In him we have redemption through his blood, the forgiveness of sins" (v. 7).

Rescue and redemption

Our rescue has come in the form of redemption. In the ancient world, to redeem something was to rescue it from captivity. The great example in the Old Testament was God's redeeming his people from slavery in Egypt. In Paul's day, slaves could be redeemed by friends and relatives—brought out of captivity by payment.

That we needed redemption again says something quite unflattering about us. We were not free. We were captives.

Sin did not just feature prominently in our lives; it controlled them. Jesus himself said, "Everyone who sins is a slave to sin" (John 8:34), and we were completely under sin's sway.

If I wrap a fine cotton thread once around my fingers, I can quickly snap it off. If I wrap the same thread around a thousand times, even though the thread itself is not very strong, the cumulative effect will be that my fingers are bound fast. Similarly, an individual sin—a little lie, a moment of greed, a fleeting lustful thought—might not feel very serious. But the reality is that every single time we sin, we bind ourselves more tightly to it. We become trapped.[1] It has happened to all of us. We are all helpless.

We need to be set free. And that is what we have in Christ. Through his perfect life, substitutionary death, and bodily resurrection we have been freed—redeemed.

Rescue and revelation

But there is more to it than that. As well as redemption we have received revelation. We are not just forgiven in an arm's-length kind of way. We have a relationship with God and are given access to some privileged information: "And he made known to us the mystery of his will, according to his good pleasure, which he purposed in Christ" (v. 9).

We have been told the "mystery of God's will." It is helpful to know that the Bible uses the word *mystery* differently from how it is often used today. In the Bible, *mystery* is not something that's too complicated to be understood. It is something that was hidden but has now been revealed. The effect is similar to that of unwrapping a birthday present. You might guess from the shape and feel that it is some kind of book or DVD or bottle. But it is only when the wrapping comes off that it is properly revealed.

There is a sense in which God's will has been hidden but is

now revealed in the gospel. Through the saving work of Jesus we get a sense of where everything is now heading. What God has done in us is bound up with what he is doing in the whole cosmos: "to bring all things in heaven and on earth together under one head, even Christ" (v. 10). That's the big picture— for our confused, fractured, and rebellious world to be aligned, healed, and restored under the loving reign of Jesus.

This underlines something we constantly need to be reminded of: God's work is about far more than me. My coming to faith is not the final goal of all God's plans. The gospel is about what he is doing with the whole of creation and all of reality. Everything is to be ordered under Jesus. All things were made by him, all things are held together by him. And one day all things will be united together under him. I am not just saved *by* him but saved *for* him. The gospel is ultimately for his sake, not mine. He will be supreme over creation. Everything will find its true place and will finally fit together under him. That's where it's all heading. Having pointed us back to our being chosen by the Father in eternity past, Paul snaps our attention forward to eternity future. And while we try to recover from the theological whiplash, we're reminded that our place in all of this comes though being "in Christ." Our Father-bestowed, Spirit-wrought blessing all comes to us as those who have, by faith, been folded into the Son.

It is worth bearing in mind where Paul is when he's writing all this.

He's not in the private library of a leading theological college. He is not writing from a Swiss mountain chalet or a beach condo in Thailand. He's not sending this letter out from the vast manicured campus of Apostle Paul International Ministries.

He is writing this as a prisoner of the Roman Empire. Not Paul the jet-setting Christian celebrity, but Paul the prisoner—for your sake (Eph. 3:1). He was most likely bound to a guard. Imagine that. He couldn't even go for a quick pee without having to take along several feet of clunking metal chain and a large Italian soldier. And yet that is not what dominates his perspective. It is not the focus of this letter. For Paul, what is most defining for us as Christians is not that we are in prison or in debt or in love or in turmoil or in want or in wealth. It is that we are in Christ. In him we have received every spiritual blessing that's available.

And it is all for the praise of God's glory (Eph. 1:12). For how the death of Christ has rescued us and how, through it, God's plan has been revealed to us, let us tumble onto our knees in adoration and thanks. Praise God for the Son!

SEALED WITH THE SPIRIT

Paul takes his readers through the chronology of how they have come to be God's people. They were predestined and chosen (v. 11). They then heard the "word of truth," the gospel, and, as they believed it, they were "included in Christ," joined to him by faith and thereafter forever bound up with him (v. 13). And having been joined to Christ, they were sealed in him with the Holy Spirit: "Having believed, you were marked in him with a seal, the promised Holy Spirit, who is a deposit guaranteeing our inheritance until the redemption of those who are God's possession—to the praise of his glory" (vv. 13–14).

We reflected earlier on something of what this means. As believers, we enjoy the presence of the Holy Spirit in our lives—a presence that assures us we are indeed children of God and that moves us to call on him in prayer. There is much more we might say about the impact and work of the Spirit on and in our lives, but Paul's focus here seems to be on how, through the Spirit, we have been marked out as belonging to

God. We bear the seal of his ownership. We have, if you like, been branded.

I remember as a kid having a small plastic contraption that made labels by punching out letters onto a strip of sticking tape. You'd laboriously slide the dial around for each letter, punch it out, and—once concluded—peel off the back of the tape to stick it on to things.

At that time I was evidently going through a particularly possessive phase; I would meticulously punch out "This belongs to Sam" and stick it on just about everything, from my prized model *Millennium Falcon* to pieces of furniture in my bedroom and (if I recall) the family cat.

I'd like to think that I'm beyond that now, but I realized recently that I still do it. A couple of new books arrived for me in the mail and, without even thinking about it, my reflex was to open them up and write my name on the inside. And as much as I congratulate myself that at least I'm not one of those people with a calligraphy *ex libris* stamp, I'm not a huge amount better. I'm still possessive.

When it comes to God, we are not just his adopted children and reconciled friends. He owns us. In fact, as soon as we become his possessions he immediately marks us as belonging to him. We have received his seal of ownership, the Holy Spirit.

We may not feel wild about being someone's property—even if that someone is God—but here's why this is wonderful. God has chosen us, taken us, and stamped us as his. And it's all for a wonderful reason. We have been chosen and adopted "in accordance with his pleasure and will" (v. 5). Notice he has revealed his plans to us "according to his good pleasure" (v. 9).

See the point? God was *pleased* to rescue us. It wasn't just some good deed of the day, the worthy chore gotten out of the way before moving on to the fun stuff. God is *pleased* to have us as his possession.

So encourage yourself with this thought: you are God's present to himself.

If I have to make a lengthy shopping trip—buying Christmas presents or getting a load of necessary-but-dull stuff for the house—I'll reward myself with a present that's for me. A treat of some kind. Something I'll look forward to enjoying once I've kicked off my shoes back home.

That is what we are to God: his present to himself. He didn't need to have us. We're not fulfilling a need in him. He has purchased us for his sheer pleasure. So much so that he put his mark of ownership on us the moment we became his. We have been sealed in Christ with the Spirit, marked as God's. We are his forever. No one and nothing will snatch us from him.

> We are his forever. No one and nothing will snatch us from him.

Again, this is all for the praise of God's glory (v. 14). So reflect on the gift of the Spirit's presence in your life, rejoice that this presence marks you out as one whom God now possesses for his sheer pleasure, and give him praise and worship!

This has been a brief look at a wonderful passage and a short book on a wonderful doctrine. In both cases we have only scratched the surface. I suggest you spend a good amount of time with the Scriptures we have looked at together, and especially this passage from Ephesians 1.

A few months ago I had what was probably the tastiest meal of my life. I was visiting some friends in America. A parent of one of them had decided to join us and had brought along with him some steaks. Good steaks. *Really* good steaks. My friend pointed out that his dad had bought them from one of the best steak companies in the country. If I saw the price I would probably mistake it for the company's phone number. We rubbed some spices into the steaks and fired them up on the outside grill. Served them with whipped potatoes and fried asparagus. I can still taste it now, and my mouth is actually watering thinking about it.

That was a meal I ate in a different way from normal. Ordinarily I tend to eat fast. Not this time. I took time over it. Each forkful was carefully selected. I savored each mouthful, allowing myself to linger over all the flavors and make the most of them. (Man, this has made me hungry!)

Some meals are worth slowing down for. And, for me, the scriptural equivalent of that steak supper is Ephesians 1:3–14. It is not a passage to wolf down before dashing off to do something else. It's a switch-off-the-phone-and-take-your-time passage. Linger over the flavors. Take small, deliberate mouthfuls. Savor the truth that the Father himself chose you before time itself came into existence. Savor the love of Christ that would compel him to come to you as a Savior, gladly rescuing you by his redemptive death. And savor the seal with which you have been marked as God's own possession—the wonderful presence of the Holy Spirit.

And as you savor these priceless flavors, let them fill your heart with thanks and adoration for God the Trinity: Father, Son, and Holy Spirit!

NOTES

Acknowledgments

1. Tim Chester, *Delighting in the Trinity* (Surrey, UK: The Good Book Company, 2011); Fred Sanders, *The Deep Things of God: How The Trinity Changes Everything* (Wheaton, IL: Crossway, 2010); Fred Sanders, *Embracing The Trinity: Life With God in the Gospel* (Nottingham, UK: IVP, 2010); Bruce A. Ware, *Father, Son, and Holy Spirit: Relationships, Roles, and Relevance* (Wheaton, IL: Crossway, 2005); Robert Letham, *The Holy Trinity: In Scripture, History, Theology, and Worship* (Phillipsburg, NJ: P&R Publishing, 2004).

2. Michael Reeves, *Delighting in the Trinity: An Introduction to the Christian Faith* (Downer's Grove, IL: IVP Academic, 2012).

Introduction

1. Michael Reeves, "Enjoying the Trinity," *UCCF*, accessed October 25, 2011, http://www.theologynetwork.org/christian-beliefs/doctrine-of-god/getting-stuck-in/enjoying-the-trinity-1--a-delight fully-different-god.htm.

2. Quoted by Robert Letham from a personal email from Ferguson in Letham, *The Holy Trinity: In Scripture, History, Theology, and Worship* (Phillipsburg, NJ: P&R Publishing, 2004), 1.

1. God: The Bottom Line

1. 50; no idea; 8 (12 if you count the "dwarf" planets like Pluto).

2. Tim Chester, *Delighting in the Trinity* (Surrey, UK: The Good Book Company, 2011), 28.

2. Divine Integrity

1. I am grateful to Tim Chester for this analogy. See *Delighting in the Trinity* (Surrey, UK: The Good Book Company, 2011), 26.

2. For the benefit of American readers, an English person nodding his head in agreement is the equivalent of a loud "whoop," and nodding vigorously—especially if accompanied by a "hmm" sound—is the equivalent of firing off several rounds of ammo into the air.

3. Instrumental in gravity overcoming the proverbial penny were John Woodhouse, "The Preacher and the Living Word," *When God's Voice Is Heard: The Power of Preaching*, ed. Christopher Green and David Jackman (Nottingham, UK: IVP, 2003), 44–45, and Chester, *Delighting in the Trinity*, 30–31.

4. A favorite term of Jesus for describing the Spirit (see John 14:17).

5. Chester, *Delighting in the Trinity*, 31.

6. Hebrews 9:14.

7. You can read about this in Mark 7:9–13.

8. For example, in Ephesians 5:18.

9. Colossians 4:6; 1 Peter 3:15.

10. Galatians 6:10; James 1:27.

3. The One Who Is Three

1. "NZ judge orders 'odd' name change," *BBC News*, last modified July 24, 2008, http://news.bbc.co.uk/1/hi/7522952.stm.

2. With one exception. I spent my first year at a university in a section of accommodation designated for women students. The university authorities had not met me and, owing to the androgynous nature of the name "Sam," were faced with a 50/50 choice.

3. Fred Sanders, *Embracing the Trinity: Life with God in the Gospel* (Nottingham, UK: IVP, 2011), 62.

4. Luke 2:40; John 4:6; Matthew 21:18; 11:19.

5. Luke 23:26.

6. Luke 2:52; Mark 5:30; John 13:21; 11:35; Matthew 26:38.

7. Mark 14:62.

8. John 8:58.

9. John 10:30.

10. Acts 5:3–4.

11. Sanders, *Embracing the Trinity*, 35.

4. The Party That Never Ends

1. C. S. Lewis, *Mere Christianity* (1952; repr., New York: HarperCollins, 2002), 174.

2. Fred Sanders, *Embracing the Trinity: Life with God in the Gospel* (Nottingham, UK: IVP, 2011), 96, 165.

5. You: An Introduction

1. The title of my friend Michael Jensen's book, *You: An Introduction* (Youngstown, OH: Matthias Media, 2008).

2. Wayne Grudem, *Evangelical Feminism and Biblical Truth: An Analysis of 118 Disputed Questions* (Nottingham, UK: IVP, 2004), 26.

3. Tim Chester, *Delighting in the Trinity* (Surrey, UK: The Good Book Company, 2011), 165.

4. *Up in the Air*, Paramount Pictures, 2009.

5. Ibid.

6. Broughton Knox, "The Everlasting God," *The Collected Works of D. Broughton Knox, Vol. 1: The Doctrine of God*, ed. Tony Payne (Youngtown, OH: Matthias Media, 2000), 155.

7. Genesis 1:5, 8, 10.

8. Genesis 2:19.

9. Genesis 2:21–22.

10. This is not to suggest that we are all to be married, as though our being a man or a woman could not be fulfilled otherwise. Jesus himself was single, and no less a man for being so.

11. Wayne Grudem, *Bible Doctrine: Essential Teachings of the Christian Faith* (Grand Rapids: Zondervan, 1999), 121–22. This insight helps to answer the question of why God did not create humanity in three different genders, rather than two, to reflect the Trinity.

12. *Vanilla Sky*, Paramount Pictures, 2001.

13. For example, in Mark 7:21.

14. See, for example, Alex Tylee, *Walking with Gay Friends: A Journey of Informed Compassion* (Nottingham, UK; IVP, 2007), and the testimonies included in *What Some of You Were: Stories About Christians and Homosexuality*, ed. Christopher Keane (Youngstown, OH: Matthias Media, 2001). The *True Freedom Trust* (www .truefreedomtrust.co.uk) has an excellent ministry among Christians facing this issue.

6. You May Now Serve the Bride

1. Eric Schlosser, *Fast Food Nation* (New York: Penguin, 2002), 130–31.

2. Robert Letham, *The Holy Trinity* (Phillipsburg, NJ: P&R Publishing, 2004), 445.

3. The words translated (in the NIV) as "man" and "woman" can also mean "husband" and "wife" (as in the ESV). There is some discussion about whether Paul primarily has marriage relationships in mind or whether he is talking about male/female relationships more generally. I am inclined to favor the latter. Briefly, Paul seems to be addressing public/church matters more than home matters, and issues that relate to "all men" and "all women," rather than just husbands and wives. Most interpretations that favor the husband/wife view still acknowledge that there is a wider, more general application.

4. Bruce A. Ware, *Father, Son, and Holy Spirit: Relationships, Roles, and Relevance* (Wheaton, IL: Crossway, 2005), 43.

5. Translation: 1988 English language ecumenical version.

6. C. S. Lewis, *Mere Christianity* (1952; repr., New York: HarperCollins, 2002), 157–58.

7. Ware, *Father, Son, and Holy Spirit*, 74 (emphasis his).

8. Wayne Grudem, *Evangelicalism and Biblical Truth* (Nottingham, UK: Apollos, 2005), 26.

9. Ibid., 26n5.

10. Kathy Keller, "Embracing the Other," in Timothy Keller with Kathy Keller, *The Meaning of Marriage* (New York: Dutton, 2011), 180.

11. It goes without saying that there are a number of details in this passage that are hard for us to understand. (Just when we thought things couldn't get more complicated, Paul drops in a reference to "the angels.")

7. Showing God to the World

1. I owe this insight, along with the phrase itself, to G. K. Beale, *We Become What We Worship* (Nottingham, UK: IVP, 2008).

2. See Romans 12:3–8; Ephesians 4:11–13; 1 Peter 4:10–11.

3. If memory serves, Hillary Clinton used it a lot in her 1990s Senate campaign.

4. Aaron Sorkin and Allsion Abner, "War Crimes," *The West Wing*, season 3, episode 5, directed by Alex Graves, aired November 7, 2001. I'm grateful to my friend Marcus Honeysett for pointing this out. (I'm also a little ashamed not to have found it myself!)

5. Kevin DeYoung and Ted Kluck, *Why We Love the Church: In Praise of Institutions and Organized Religion* (Chicago: Moody, 2009), 12.

8. What Really Happens When You Talk to God

1. English actors seem to have cornered the market on this one. See any movie starring Hugh Grant.

2. George McFly in *Back to the Future.*

3. I think they did this with Steve Martin's character in *Roxanne.*

4. C. S. Lewis, *Letters to Malcolm* (1963; repr., San Diego: Harcourt, 1992), 113.

5. This illustration comes from Tim Keller.

6. Lewis, *Letters to Malcolm,* 68.

7. Fred Sanders, *Embracing the Trinity: Life with God in the Gospel* (Nottingham, UK: IVP, 2011), 215.

8. Ronald Dunn, *Don't Just Stand There . . . Pray Something!* (Grand Rapids: Zondervan, 2003), 33.

9. To the Praise of Father, Son, and Holy Spirit

1. This illustration comes from a talk by Tim Keller.

ALSO BY SAM ALLBERRY

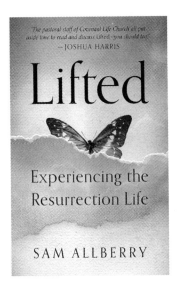

Sam Allberry shows us that the resurrection is far more than a mere event. It isn't just for Easter; it has overwhelmingly positive implications for our lives every day.

The resurrection gives us real assurance of forgiveness and salvation, power to live new and transformed lives, and hope for life after death. Our lives are now different; we have been *lifted*. Read and be transformed by the real significance of the resurrection.

"Full of great images, clearly organized, encouraging, humorous, biblical, insightful—I could go on. Reading this little volume on this central but neglected topic will benefit your life."
  —*Mark Dever,* Capitol Hill Baptist Church